11 Years 9 Months, and 5 Days

11 YEARS 9 MONTHS, AND 5 DAYS

Burger Store Episodes and Frustrations

GREG TATE

1979-VARN

Library of Congress Number: 00-191611

ISBN #: Hardcover 0-7388-2983-8

Softcover 0-7388-2984-6

This book was printed in the United States of America.

To order additional copies of this book, contact:

Xlibris Corporation

1-888-7-XLIBRIS

www.Xlibris.com

Orders@Xlibris.com

CONTENTS

Acknowledgements

I would like to thank Sue Hayden, for giving me the title to my book. Love you much. Many thanks to my best friend, Steve Ribbleton, for letting me use his computer, to type my book. I love you man. Also, many thanks to my good friends, Cody Foucher and Geoff Dybert. I love you guys. Lots of thanks to my good friend, Fred Raulsten, who reminded me that, life's too short to mill around, go on and do it.

Introduction

This book is about the time I worked at the Burger Store on Jedsen Street in Peddleton. Some of the episodes in this book are unbelievable. The people's names in this book are totally fictional. During my time at the Burger Store, I saw a lot of people come and go. You will witness certain people's names appearing not only once, but many times. That just means that person was involved in that episode. This book contains its share of profanity. Some of it intense. Now that I've given you fair warning, let's get to the first chapter.

1979-VARN

Chapter 1

1985-1986

It's September 7, 1985. My first day working at the Burger Store as a janitor. The first thing I had to do was clean the stairs. I told manager Cheryl Krepps I was going to clean the stairs. She (angry) said, "Do it!" I thought, "You ungrateful bitch." That's just one of the many stories you will witness as you read this book.

About a week later, Joel Alaveda was mopping at the feet of Dale Karvis. That made Dale mad. Matt Praffer and Craig Girnett had to drag Dale downstairs to keep from hitting Joel.

Two weeks later, assistant manager Jed Toyce jumped Dale's case because he was salting the big burgers wrong or something. Matt and Jerry Alaveda had to carry Dale downstairs to keep him from hitting Jed with a meat spatula.

A week after that, Randall Tarks asked me a question. Store manager Ward Barick jumped on my case for answering Randall's question. If someone asks me a question, I'm going to answer it if I can.

One day in late October, I had all my work finished .Jed was questioning me if I had it all finished. He was being snotty when questioning me. He asked me if I had all my work done. I said, "Yes." He then says "Do you"? I got right in his face and said, "Yeah! Don't you trust me?" He just looked at me and said, "Go ahead and go." It was time for me to go anyway. A week later, Jed got transferred to the Long Branch store. I was glad to see him go.

The Burger Store had an inspection in April 1986. Craig had not shaved. The Burger Store required employees to be clean shaven. Ward went to a nearby store to get a razor and shave cream. He made Craig shave.

A few days later, Dean Merker was hired. Dean turned out to be a good worker. However, a few weeks later, Dean quit. A customer complained about a blonde hair being on their fries. Dean got blamed for it. Dean had blonde hair but he wasn't working the fries. He wasn't anywhere near the fries. Dean was working at the grills. Ward accused Dean of causing that blonde hair on that customer's fries. That really pissed Dean off. I didn't blame Dean one bit.

A month and a half later, someone on night shift stole the VCR out of the break room. It had to have been night shift. There were too many people during the day shift to do it. A few days later, the store got another VCR. However, that day the new VCR was bolted down. Someone actually loosened the bolts to try and steal the new VCR. They were unsuccessful.

I remember one day in late June, Terry Croyce told me to reach down in the toilet and pull something out of it. I told him, "I'm not doing it." I don't know what it was he wanted me to pull out of the toilet. I wasn't going to do it. I didn't. At about the same time, Jed was fired from the Burger Store. He stole $77 from a cash register. Actually, the money fell out of the register onto the floor. Someone saw him pocket the money and reported it. He was fired a day later.

The first week of July had arrived. That first Saturday, Lyle Grobe, the owner of the Burger Store came in that day. He asked me if I knew how to operate the grills. I said, "No sir." He (angry) said, "The next time I come in, you better know how to work the grills." I thought, "You asshole." I was never shown how to operate the grills.

A week later, the basement flooded. I asked assistant manager Tawney Roggins if I could have some help. The water was about 6 inches deep. She asked Ward but he said no. It took me almost 4 hours to clean up the flood.

A couple of weeks later, I had scrubbed the drive-thru pad that morning. Lyle came in about 2 hours later. He was griping as usual. Apparently, he complained about the drive-thru pad. So, Cheryl tells me that Lyle wants me to scrub the drive-thru pad. I told her, "I already scrubbed it."

She said, "He wants you to do it again." I got mad and said, "I hate that son of a bitch." Cheryl just walked away. Lyle was definitely on my bad list.

During the last week of July, a leak had occurred in the break room. It was one of the pipes that was leaking. It would continue to leak for a long time.

One day during the second week of August, Nora Bachtold had been really sick. She asked Chasity Minsted if she could go home. Chasity said, "Go downstairs and gather some Large Burger boxes." Nora was throwing up and about to pass out. Chasity still insisted that Nora gather Large Burger boxes. Chasity never did let Nora go home early. It seemed like Chasity changed when she got promoted as a swing manager. Nora complained about what had happened. That never happened to Nora again.

One Sunday in August, the truck didn't arrive until 1:45 PM. It was supposed to arrive at 4:15 AM. Brett Swasher and I had already left. Dale and Ronald McGroast were left to unload the truck. The next day, Brett said they did a horrible job of unloading. They stacked new stock on old stock. They didn't rotate anything. I can see why they did a horrible job. Dale and Ronald never got along. I remember one time, Dale told Ronald, "Stay out of my kitchen." Ronald said "This is the Burger Store, not Dale's store."

In early October, someone on night shift cleaned the grill with the brand new window squeegee. Brett was getting ready to clean the windows when he noticed the squeegee had grease on it. Brett got mad and said, "Them mother fuckers". A week later, someone on night shift splattered grease on the wall under the cabinet. I had cleaned that wall a day earlier. Brett and I got mad and said, "Them fuckers".

The first Sunday in November, Dale and I were scheduled to unload truck. Dale was not told that the schedule had changed. They had originally scheduled Dale and I to unload truck. I looked at the schedule that morning. It said that Jay Cloover and I were supposed to unload truck. Jay had never unloaded truck. Dale had unloaded truck several times. Although, he never did do it right. He never rotated the stock. The change in the schedule made Dale mad. He walked out at 5:45 AM.

In mid December, the local pest control was spraying for bugs. Everything was covered up so the pesticide wouldn't get on the food sur-

1979-VARN

faces. There was nothing my co-workers could do. They couldn't cook anything cause the pesticide might get on the food. Chasity called Ward and told him what was happening. Ward came in at 5:30 that morning. When he got there, he jumped everybody's case. He cussed Chasity left and right. The store was suppose to open at 6:00 AM. It didn't get opened until 6:45 AM. He told Chris Beffords to go make biscuits right away. Brett had not shown up yet. Ward told Chasity to call me in to work. Chris heard what Ward said. Chris said to himself, "Uh-oh! Greg's not going to like that." Chasity tried calling but could not get a hold of me. My mom had already left for work that morning. I was asleep and didn't hear the phone ring. I had just come off working 8 straight days. I was very tired. Brett finally showed up at 9:30 that morning. The same day, Lou Driese was supposed to be off work that day for court. He told Tawney he needed to be off that day (Friday). He told her that in the office. She had the schedule right there with her too. The thing is, Tawney forgot to mark him off the schedule. Lou was scheduled to be in at 10:00 AM. He showed up an hour and a half late. Lou told Ward that he had court that day. Ward (angry) said, "I don't want to hear what you have to say, that's between you and Tawney. You might even get fired for this." Thankfully, Lou did not get fired. That was one messed up day.

Chapter 2

1987

The new year had arrived. January didn't start out to pretty though. It was on a Thursday morning. I noticed something stunk in the basement. Someone on night shift had shit in the mop bucket. They even threw their toilet paper in the trash can. I told Ward but he said, "Clean it anyway." A minute later, Craig took one step on the stairs and said, "Oh God". I told him they shit in the mop bucket. I had to clean it 30 times before it started smelling half way descent.

A month and a half later, Mike Dalls got sent on break after being at work for just 24 minutes. A month and a half after that, Alex Karvis was an hour late for work. Alex was always on time. Someone changed the sched ule and didn't tell or call him. Well, Ward got mad at him. I remember Ward (angry) saying to Alex, "Get in the kitchen". Alex called in sick a week later. He must have been sick. It wasn't like Alex to call in sick. Employees were required to call 2 hours before their scheduled shift if they were sick. Alex called in 4 hours before his shift. He called at 6:00 AM. He did that so Ward wouldn't catch him. Ward came in at 7:00 AM. Ward and Alex did not get along at all.

A week later, the power went out that morning. Chasity had not shown up yet. She was supposed to open that morning. Ward got there and said, "What is her fucking problem?" We also had truck that day. Brett and I wound up unloading the truck in the dark. Chasity worked the next day. I asked her what happened. She looked at the schedule wrong. She thought she was off that day. It was the next week that day she was off.

During the last part of April, Jennilee Sibbs learned how to cook. She had mainly worked front line and drive-thru. In early May, she found another job at a shoe store. It paid more than the Burger Store. When Ward found out, he was mad. Ward said to Jennilee, "You mean I wasted my time showing you how to do everything and you find another job?" I thought if she had a chance at a better job, then go for it.

The first week of June, night shift was leaving trash bags beside the dumpster. Trash bags were supposed to be put inside the dumpster. Brett was pissed off about trash bags not being put inside the dumpster. He said he was going to leave a note on the dumpster. I asked him what he was going to write. He said he was going to say, "Hey you dumb asses, throw the trash bags in the dumpster." He never got to it so I wrote that note. The note said, "Hey you dumb asses, trash bags go inside the dumpster, not beside it or behind it." The note worked for one night. The problem was, the lady next door didn't like the note because it said, "dumb asses." I had to take it down. Night shift kept on leaving trash bags beside the dumpster. Maury Kolmes said that there were 11 bags of trash left out by the dumpster one time. A few days later , they finally stopped leaving trash bags by the dumpster.

It was June 11, Brett quit the Burger Store. I hated to see him go. We were a good team. When he left, I was the head janitor. Other problems were taking place in June. The first week, customers would not flush the toilet. That really pissed me off. I left a note saying, "Please flush the toilet. Also, do not put tons and tons of paper in the toilet, or it will overflow. This is a must." That note did not work. So I wrote another note saying, "It is disgusting to see a toilet overflow, especially if it has turds in it. How would you like it if I stopped up your toilet and it overflowed? You wouldn't like it would you ? So don't do it to me." The note worked for a while until someone took it down. Then, someone didn't flush the toilet. I left yet another note. This note said, "Do you think it's disgusting to see turds in a toilet? There is a handle on this toilet to make the turds disappear. If God wanted to let turds sit in the toilet and stink up the place, he would not have put a handle on this toilet to make the turds disappear. So please flush the toilet, this is a must." That note seemed to have worked. Another problem was a couple of rude customers. One Thursday during the second week of June, Maury was walking by the drive-thru speaker. A woman pulled up and said, "Get you ass in there and tell them to take my order." Maury ignored her. It was 10 minutes before we opened. Just a few minutes later, some guy pulled up 5 minutes before we opened. He started saying "Them mother fuckers, them mother fuckers." I thought, "OooK!" Night shift caused me one problem the third week of June. Someone punctured a carton of caramel sundae topping. It leaked onto the shelf. The puncture was caused by someone sticking a pen or pencil into the carton. The puddle of sundae topping was about a foot and a half in diameter. Of course, I had to clean it up.

The Burger Store had a storage corral that was outside next to the freezer. The grease disposal and empty bun trays were inside the corral. During June, I just happened to see a rat in the corral. I felt I needed to kill that rat. I put weed killer on a biscuit. The rat ate it. I never did see that rat again. My supervisor Keith Parden said that rat probably had a family out there. I said, "Tough".

In late July, Ward did something disgusting. He was walking towards the counter. He suddenly stopped and farted. He said, "Excuse me" sarcastically. I thought, "You could've been more polite."

Mark Grobe, Lyle's son was now the owner of the Burger Store. Lyle signed all of his Burger Stores over to Mark. Lyle was getting up in age. In case he died, he didn't want Mark to have to buy them back from the corporation. Lyle had 5 stores. On August 15, Christa Shirbin quit. Mark came by that day. He said, "How are you doing Christa?" She said, "I'm doing great. I'm quitting." Mark said, "Why are you quitting?" Christa said, "I'm tired of all this damn bullshit." Mark said, "OK."

During August, everybody was trying to get rid of Ward. He played favorites. He had Janie Malder , Candy Rackson, and Samantha Korsman wrapped around his finger because they were good looking. He didn't like Ola Bachtold or Andrea Hewsley because they were black. They were good workers. Ward didn't like Craig because he knew a lot about the store. He knew just as much as Ward did. Craig may have even known a little more. Craig quit during the third week of August. Bob Hotson was tired of the way Ward was doing things. Sometime during August, he sent the store office a letter. The letter said, Dear Mark Grobe, My co-workers and I have a problem with Ward. He plays favorites and doesn't like blacks. He has the good looking women wrapped around his finger. He does not treat the good workers fair. Whenever the store runs out of a product, we tell him right away. He says he's going to order it. Then as time goes by, we are still out of a certain product. We tell him again and he gets mad and says why didn't you tell me? I just feel Ward is not a good store manager. Sincerely Concerned Employee Bob had the letter typed. That way no one could detect his hand writing. Employees started calling the store office complaining about Ward. I remember asking Andrea about Ward. She said, "We're going to get rid of that bald headed mother fucker." I also remember hearing Keith saying that, "Whoever is calling the office complaining about Ward needs to stop." It went on for a little while. It eventually stopped.

It was August 27, the store had an inspection that day. Rodney Sturwin was the inspector. Rusty Fluett and I were working that day. Well, I was on break at the time. Rusty was on the clock. Chasity asked me to throw away one case of expired milk. I told her, "I'm was on break. Rusty is still on the clock." She said, "Would you come throw this milk away?" I wound up having to throw that milk away. I got angry and said, "Son of a bitch, I don't know why I have to throw away this mother fucking shit." No one said a word after I had that tantrum.

In late August, I was checking the men's restroom. All of a sudden I heard somebody in the stall saying, "Oooooh! Dolly!" I thought, "OooK!" On August 30, Alex quit the Burger Store. Although, The schedule said he was terminated. Ward also said he was terminated. Alex drove up and I said, "Hello Alex, I heard you got terminated?" He said "What"? I told him that's what the schedule said. Ward said you were also terminated. Alex said, "He can kiss my terminated ass. I told him I quit." Alex turned in his uniforms and left. He squealed his tires as he left. I didn't blame him. Ward always treated Alex like crap. When employees have days off from work, if someone was to call them in to work. They have the right to say no. But in Alex's case, whenever someone would call him in whether it be Ward or whoever. If Alex said no, Ward would tell him or tell whoever was calling Alex, they would say, "Either come in or get fired." He had called in a couple of times. The only thing was, whenever he tried to call in, Ward or whoever Alex was talking to would say, "You can't call in, you will be fired." Alex, both times called in at least 2 or 3 hours before his scheduled shift. When he called in, I know he was sick. I remember because Alex would only call in if he was really sick. I sure hated to see Alex leave. He was a good worker.

A few days after Labor Day, I had to get ice for front line. There were 9 people working front counter. It was fairly busy. Assistant manager Lauren Pallick said, "There are 9 people working front counter and you have to get ice?" I said, "I guess so." I guess everybody on front line was lazy. A week later, I was on break. I was getting my food together. Suddenly, Tawney tells me to bring up salads. I told her I was on break. Chasity(angry) tells me, "Do it!" I had to interrupt my break to get salads. When I was walking back to the cooler, I had a tantrum. I yelled, "I'm so damn tired of this mother fucking place." No one said a word. It was a good thing.

During September, Nicky Balters had been stealing cases of burgers from the freezer. He was going to get fired, but he quit before they could fire him. There for a while, I had to have a manager go out to the freezer with me. That way they could keep an eye on me. They knew that I wasn't the one that was stealing. A lot of times, I couldn't get any managers to go, They were too busy. I remember one time I needed to go to the freezer. I had asked Ward but he got mad. This having a manager going to the freezer with me was not going to work. The last week of September, Wardell Tullen and I found a whiskey bottle in the toilet. We suspected it was a wino from Hemstead Court that put it there.

In October, Hannah Mylend was having more trouble with Lauren. They never did get along. Lauren had a reputation of being a slave driver. Lauren was constantly picking at Hannah. Hannah was a good worker. One time Lauren threatened to fire her. Hannah went to Ward immediately. Lauren could not fire anybody. All she could do was hire. The first week of October, the toilet in the men's restroom had a part that was broke. Lauren told me to fix it. I told her I didn't know how to fix it. Lauren said, "You don't?" She then said, "How do you expect to be a husband if you can't fix the toilet?" I said, "That's a plumber's job." I thought, "What the hell does fixing a toilet have to do with being a husband?" Later that day, Ross Klurry from the store office came to fix the toilet. I was surprised he did. He was known not to do his job. I thought about what Lauren had said to me. I thought, "You dumb bitch." I wasn't even going with anybody. I wasn't even thinking about getting married. Even if I was married, I would call a plumber to fix the toilet. A few days later, Ross refused to come and fix the washing machine. Lyle fired him. Three days later, Lyle hired him back. After all, Ross was Lyle's son-in-law. Ross was married to Lyle's daughter Sally. The day Ross got hired back, he came by and tried to fix the washing machine. It was so old it couldn't be fixed. A few days later, Mark bought a brand new washing machine.

Hannah continued to have trouble with Lauren. I remember one time a customer brought back an order that was incorrect. Hannah was taking care of it. However, she did not wait on that customer. To make matters worse, Lauren comes over to see what the problem is. Lauren found out and yelled at Hannah like there was no tomorrow. Hannah was really embarrassed. Hannah (angry) said, "You just embarrassed me". Lauren (angry) said "That's too bad". One time Hannah was needing a ride home. We had both worked the same shift that day. It wasn't any trouble, we were neighbors. Well, Lauren found out I was giving Hannah a ride home. She said, "Oooooh!" Lauren acted like Hannah and I had something going. We were just friends. I remember on the way home, Hannah said, "If Lauren dies, I'm going to send her some black roses."

The last Sunday in October, the truck ran that day. I was scheduled to work from 4:15 AM to 9:00 AM. I got to work and found out that Chip Bronston had no transportation to work. Chip was supposed to help me unload truck. Well, I was left to unload truck by myself. Also, Jay, Lonnie Arnsburg, and I had plans to go ice skating that day. Somehow, I lucked out and got to leave at 9:00 AM. However, Chip didn't even get wrote up for not coming into work. The next day, I was checking the men's restroom. All of a sudden some guy started saying, "Gina! Gina! Gina!" I thought, "OK."

An unfortunate thing happened to Hannah the first week of November. Her drawer came up $2 short. It was the first time her drawer had come up short. Tawney found out and reported it to Ward. Tawney said she would let Hannah know if Ward was going to fire her. The next day, Hannah got a call that morning from Tawney. She told Hannah, "Ned said you're fired." Hannah said, "That's fine, fuck you." A week later, Hannah came in and got her last check. Rita, Hannah's sister, came in and said to manager Dena Gurp, "You fire all the good people and keep all the bad people." I didn't blame Rita for saying that at all. Although it didn't make me look good. I could've cared less.

The Sunday before Thanksgiving, the truck ran that day. Chip and I were scheduled to unload truck that day. Chip didn't show up for work. Nobody left a note saying he wasn't going to make it to work. He just didn't show up for work. Dena called him and asked him why he had not shown up for work. Chip said, "Depression, I guess." I thought, "If depression was the case, hell I'd never show up for work." I also had plans to go ice skating that day. I didn't exactly get off at 9:00 AM like the schedule said. I did get off at 11:30 AM. I still got to go ice skating. This time, Chip got wrote up for no-showing. Which was exactly right.

The last week of November, the Burger Store changed the way call ins were made. The opening employees had to call in the night before their shift. I thought, "How do you know if you're going to be sick when you get up in the morning?" Somctimes you can wake up sick. Well, that way didn't last long at all.

The day before Thanksgiving, the truck ran. I was putting the sundae mix in the cooler. I had it all put up until, a box of sundae mix leaked all over the floor. I had to pull all the cases of sundae mix out of the cooler. I had to pull all the pallets out and clean the floor. I got the floor cleaned and the pallets were put back in place. I began putting the sundae mix up (again). I got the sundae mix put up until, another box of sundae mix leaked all over the floor (again). That made me so damn mad. This time, I just threw the whole damn box away. I know that one of the bags of mix was still good. At that point, I just didn't care. I began pulling the cases of sundae mix and pallets out (again). I cleaned the floor (again). I began putting the sundae mix up (again). I said to myself, "If another box of sundae mix leaks all over the floor, I'm walking out of here." I began putting the sundae mix up (again). This time, no leaks. Someone must have heard what I had said to myself. Nothing bizarre happened the rest of the year. Although, Hannah was doing some investigating in trying to get Ward fired. She was hoping to get her job back.

1979-VARN

Chapter 3

1988

Hannah continued her investigation into the new year. She was trying to find anything to get Ward fired. She somehow found out about the time when Ward said, "Come on, we need the big burgers son." She said that Mark and Keith were trying to fire Ward after what he had said to me. Apparently, he found some kind of loophole. Hannah never did get her job back.

In February, Ola got promoted to swing manager. One Sunday that month, she was the opening manager. The truck ran that day. Chip and I were scheduled to unload it. The truck driver Pete handed Ola the stock invoice. It was Ola's first time working on truck day. Chip was helping her with the invoice. However, Pete was getting mad at Chip because he wasn't helping me unload stock. Pete and Chip continued to argue. I don't know what all was said but I do remember hearing Pete say, "She can figure out how to do the invoice." Pete said that Chip needed to help me unload the truck. They continued to argue. I heard Chip say to Pete, "Your name isn't on my paychecks." I have to say I agreed with Pete. Chip should've helped me unload the truck more than he did. Ola could've figured out the invoice. Then again, Chip and Ola were going together. After Pete left, Chip was bragging to Cody Foucher about how he was going to whip Pete's ass. Chip said, "If Pete had stepped down from the truck, I was going to whip his ass."

In early March, Tawney accused Chip and me of not doing our work. She accused me more. She was threatening to take me off the schedule. She said she was going to get someone who could do the janitorial job. I know I was doing my job. Tawney was just that way. Since she became a salaried manager, she became more unfriendly. Take my word for it, not hardly anybody would work the janitor's position. Then again, Rodney was coming in the next day. That was one reason she was being more unfriendly. One day during the second week of April, Tawney told Nisha Stoss to sweep front line. As Nisha started to sweep, Tawney took the broom right out of her hands. She told Nisha to do something else. Nisha was pissed.

A week later, Dena tried to call me into work. Chip had called in sick. I told her I couldn't because I had things I had to do. Well, Ward calls me 2 hours later. He said, "Why didn't you come in and work?" I said, "I had stuff I had to do." He said, "That's why we have 2 janitors." I was supposed to have my car aligned and I was going to pay my car registration. Instead, I had to cancel those plans and go into work.

During the last week of April, Tawney called Jeanette McCrain into work at 10:00 AM. Jeanette had gotten ready and as she was walking out of the door, Tawney called her back and said they didn't need her after all. Jeanette got ready for nothing.

On April 30, Reva Pefner quit. Reva was known to call in at least once a month. She didn't have to be sick. She just didn't want to be at the Burger Store.

On the morning of May 3, Ola called me at 4:45 AM. My mom answered the phone. Ola said, "This is the Burger Store, is Greg there?" My mom said, "Chip called in sick." Ola was needing me to go in and work. My mom said that Ola was rude over the phone. She said that Ola didn't say who she was. When I got to work, Ola said that Chip injured his foot with a lawnmower and couldn't make it. The next day was my day off. Well, Dena tried to call me into work at 4:35 AM. I never did hear the phone ring. My mom however, got woke up by Dena's call. My mom was off that day too. My mom was so pissed at getting woke up. She told Dena I had gone up to my grandparent's house and spent the night. It was obvious, Chip had called in again. From May 5 to May 12, I had worked 8 straight days. Chip finally returned to work May 12. Chip told me he didn't injure his foot with a lawnmower. I realized that when he returned. He wasn't limping at all. He said he just needed that time off. He also knew I was needing some extra hours. That was true. I wound up with 108 hours for the first 2 weeks in May.

During the third week of June, Dave Jerris and Cody were in the basement having a conversation. Cody was eating a piece of bacon. Dave saw Ward coming downstairs, so Dave went back upstairs. Ward caught Cody eating the bacon. Ward asked what that was. Cody said, "It was something to eat." Ward was pissed. That piece of bacon was going to be thrown away anyway. But according to the Burger Store rules, eating expired food is considered stealing. Ward suspended Cody for a week.

That rule about having a manager going to the freezer with me was still in effect. During the last week of June, I was looking for a manager to go to the freezer with me. They said they were busy, as usual. I had asked LuAnn Callmon. Tawney comes along and says, "Jay will go." Tawney (angry) then says, "Quit wondering around the store." I was just doing what the rule said. Tawney didn't have to be hateful about it.

One day during the first week of July, Cody was washing dishes. Ward asked him why he wasn't done with the dishes. Cody said, "I still got 2 more mother fucking dishes to wash." Ward just kind of looked at him. The next day, Cody was washing dishes. Ward got onto him for not having them done. Cody said "Look mother fucker, I'm getting the dishes done." Ward did nothing. Cody would have whipped his ass. The thing about washing dishes was that you never knew if you might get called to help out in the grill area or somewhere else.

A week later, Tawney acted hateful again. She needed me to bring a water cooler to the front counter for a customer. Cody was asking me a question. Tawney told me not to talk to him. I got the water cooler and was taking it up front. Tawney (angry) says, "What are you doing?" I (angry) said, "I'm taking the cooler up front." She didn't say anything back. She had no right talking to me like that.

A few days later, Ken Beeker was on break. He had ordered a cheeseburger. Actually, he was fixing himself a double cheeseburger. Brenda Wylon caught him. She told Ward, "Ken had paid for a cheeseburger, not a double cheeseburger." Ward fired him. Ken went out the back door. Ward said, "You're not supposed to go out that door." Ken said, "Fuck you, I don't work here anymore." Robert Gellen and I, just had to laugh.

1979-VARN

During the third week in July, Tawney said I wasn't doing my job right. She said that they were not going to need me anymore. She was probably talking about Keith, Mark, and Rodney. I just let what she said go in one ear and out the other. Take my word for it, they needed me BAD. Chip had quit a few days earlier. They would not pay him at least $4 an hour. At the time, Chip and I were making about $3.70 an hour. Another reason was because Alec Roggins was on leave of absence from the National Guard.

It was Saturday, July 23. Dave was off that day. I remember him telling me a couple of days ago. He said that he was going to be off Friday and Saturday. I remember coming in that Saturday and Dave was not on the schedule. When Ward came in, he wrote Dave's name on the schedule. Ward had one of the swing managers call him. Dave showed up late that morning. I overheard Ward say to Dave, "When you're scheduled to be here, you're supposed to be here." Dave had explained that he was not scheduled to work that day. Ward would not listen and fired Dave. Ward just wanted to get rid of Dave because he was black. The Burger Store lost another damn good worker because of Ward's idiocy.

Earlier that week, Ward's car got egged. He was going to pay $50 to whoever knew who did it. At the same time, Ward was giving Kerry Mullinger a hard time. Kerry worked nights. I heard people tell me that he was a good worker. Ward had worked a few nights that week. Kerry worked the same nights as Ward. I heard that Ward was always picking at Kerry. Well, the night of July 23 Kerry worked and Ward didn't. Kerry had an idea. Kerry decided he would really get back at Ward. He put on the outside reader board, "WARD SUCKS". I thought that was so funny, along with everyone else. The next morning, Ward found out what Kerry did. He had been questioning Mike that morning. I heard Ward say to Mike, "Your job could be at stake if you don't tell me who put that on the reader board." Well, Ward got his information from Mike. He then fired Kerry. A day later, I worked my 10th day in a row. Mark asked me how I was doing. I said, "I am tired." He asked why I was tired. I said, "This is my 10th day in a row." He said, "Oh!" I bet he never had to work 10 days in a row.

It was Thursday, July 28, I got off early that day. I had heard that Kerry had planned on coming by that morning to kick Ward's ass. Somehow, Ward found out about it and called the police. Kerry had stopped by, but the police were there. Kerry had to back away.

Although this didn't happen at the Burger Store, I had seen Dave at a local convenience store on August 2. He asked me what was going on at the Burger Store. I told him that Ward's car got egged. I told him that Ward was going to pay $50 to whoever knew who did it. Dave said quickly, "Tell him I did it and I'll split the money with you half and half." Dave said, "If he tries to do anything, I'll kick his ass." I told him that Ward already found out who did it. Of course, it was Kerry. I told Dave about the reader board. We both had a good laugh.

Throughout July & August, there was a woman that came through drive-thru. Every time I was scrubbing the drive-thru pad, she would always tell me to scrub in a certain place. In mid August, she told me to scrub in a certain place. I told her, "I know how to do my job." She never said anything back to me. I never did see her again, and haven't seen her since. Also in mid August, truck driver Fred Raulsten was unloading stock at the store in Barkley. Well, Lyle was there and started griping at the employees because the truck was in the drive-thru. Lyle said, "You've got 15 minutes to unload the truck." Fred had thought, "How was I going to unload 300 pieces of stock in 15 minutes?" There was no way. Lyle was just griping like he always did.

A few days later, I was getting rid of some empty boxes. As I was getting rid of them, Tawney (angry) comes along and says, "What are you doing?" I (angry) said "I'm taking out these boxes." She then tells me to get rid of those boxes. I told her I was. She just had to be hateful.

Five days later, Cody was caught up on biscuits. Garrett Bachtold was needing help in the kitchen. Garrett said to Cody, "I need you to help me in the kitchen." Cody said, "I'm not helping your fat ass." Garrett said, "You're a damn liar too." Cody said, "I'm not helping you". Garrett called Cody a bastard. Cody said, "I'm still not helping your fat ass." Garrett then chased Cody out of the store and onto the parking lot. They were still on the clock. Garrett didn't catch him. However, Garrett could run pretty fast for his size. He weighed nearly 300 pounds. That was one episode I'll never forget. It was so funny. The managers didn't even do anything about it. Then again, they didn't see it.

A few weeks later, Robert was working his ass off. Tawney and Molly Bargman were constantly picking at him. They were saying, "Do this, do that." Finally, Robert got so angry he said, "I'm tired of your damn fucking shit."

Robert then quit. I saw Robert waiting for his ride. I asked him what happened. He told me that they had been picking at him, and he was sick of it. He said about Tawney, "Fuck her and the horse she rode in on." He said, "You can tell Molly, she's a god damn whore." A few minutes later, Tawney was saying that Robert said that he quit. Tawney said she fired him. Robert did quit. Jay saw the whole thing. Tawney was griping because of how Robert had talked to her. I felt Tawney got what she deserved. Jay and I laughed at what Robert had done. Again, the Burger Store had lost another good worker because of the managers being idiots.

A week later, someone had written on the wall, "Ward has aids and Dena gave them to him." Dena comes up to me and says, "When you see things like that, you should mark them out." I told her, "I didn't see it." Although, I really did. I thought it was funny.

A few things happened the last week of September that were really disgusting. Someone on night shift took a shit in the grease bucket. The next day, someone took a shit in an empty pickle bucket. Those buckets were used to dispose of old grease. Another thing that happened during the last week of September was a customer said that the restroom was flooded. Stan Kobes went to clean it up the flood. The problem was, there was not a drop of water on the floor. That kind of prank would happen at least 12 times before it was all said and done.

From September 20 to September 30, I worked 11 days in a row. Six of those days were 11 hour days. The pay period ended September 30. I had 122 ¾ hours on my check. That was a Burger Store record.

During the first week of October, Nina McGleary hit the fire escape switch by accident. A substance shot out and went everywhere. The substance got into the frying vats. I was cleaning out the vats and Ward (angry) said, "What are you doing?" I (angry) said, "I'm cleaning this stuff out." He didn't say anything else. It was a good thing. I was ready to knock his head off.

In mid October, Tawney hires Wes Besler as a janitor. He started out good but a week later, he started to turn bad. I was scheduled to get off at 9:00 AM on Sunday, October 23. Wes was scheduled to get off at 1:00 PM. He wanted to switch schedules with me. He said he would work until 1:00 Thursday. Well, Thursday came along and Wes called in sick. I was stuck doing truck and the rest of Wes' work by myself. You talk about being pissed.

The next day, a friend of mine, Derek Tullen was hired. However, he was fired on the same day he was hired. He was working that night. While he was on break, one of his co-workers stole a pork steak sandwich and ran downstairs to the break room. That person heard someone coming downstairs. That person went back upstairs. Derek was sitting at the table and that person left the pork steak sandwich on the table. Tawney came downstairs and saw Derek sitting at the table. Tawney accused Derek of stealing that pork steak sandwich. She fired him on the spot. Derek explained that it was that guy who ran upstairs that stole that sandwich. Tawney didn't believe him and Derek was still fired.

It was Saturday, October 29, I was supposed to be off work that day. I didn't get to sleep until 1:30 AM the night before last. I had been out visiting friends who were in from college. I was also getting ready to go on vacation. I was going to spend all day Saturday packing. However, Wes called in sick that day. Tawney calls me at 5:30 AM to tell me that Wes called in sick. Instead of having that day off, I had to go to work. My mom said, "They might try to call you while you are on vacation." I told her, "Don't you tell them what hotel I'm staying at, because they might try to call me." When I got to work, Tawney had the nerve to say, "You're mad aren't you?" I (angry) said, "You're damn right I'm mad." She told me she was going to fire Wes. It didn't happen.

The next day, the truck ran. I was scheduled to get off at 9:00 AM. Wes was scheduled until 1:00 PM. I asked him if he was feeling better. He said, "Yes". I asked Tawney if I could get off at 9:00. She said, "You sure can." When Wes and I got through unloading the truck, Wes was holding his stomach and said, "Oh! I don't think I can make it until 1:00." I went to LuAnn and said, "Wes says he can't make it until 1:00." She said, "That's tough". I was able to get off work at 9:00.

On Halloween, the pay period ended. I wound up with 101 hours. It was my third consecutive check of 100 or more hours.

I was on vacation the first week of November. I was told that on Thursday that Wes caught one of the frying vats on fire. When that happened, LuAnn said, "Oh! I wished Greg was here." That same day, someone said that Cody stayed 30 minutes over on his break. Employees were given 30 minutes for break. Ward said to Cody, "Taking these hour breaks huh!" Ward sent him home. Cody told me he only stayed 5 minutes past his break. The next day, Lauren walked out on her job. She apparently had enough of the Burger Store. That same day, Lauren's sister, Kylene, told Ward that next Friday was her last day. Ward said, "No, it's today." That same Friday was Wes' last day.

A week and a half later, Donald Vickerson was cooking pork steaks. Chasity said, "We need pork steaks cooked." Donald said, "Pork steaks are cooking." Ward (sarcastically) said, "Donald, go home." I was on break when this happened. Donald came downstairs and I said, "Is everything alright Donald?" He said, "Yeah." Then he told me what happened and punched one of the lockers. He quit the same day. I think Ward wanted to get rid of him because he was black. Once again, another good worker lost because of manager's idiocy.

A week later at about 9:45 AM, Tawney gives me a list of things she needed me to do. There was no way I was going to get that list done by 1:00 PM. When 11:15 AM rolled around, she sent me home. I said, "What about that list?" She said, "Do it some other time, labor's high." I said, "Well!"

During November, Cody had his hours cut drastically. He was only getting 2 days a week. That continued for quite a while. Cody would have to find a second job. The reason why he had his hours cut is because he was black. Cody was only getting 16 hours a week. Ward had hired Fonda Kresp as a biscuit maker. I guess Ward thought that she would be better than Cody. Guess what? Ward was wrong. Cody was a better worker. Fonda was lazy as hell.

On November 30, Kip Derkowitz quit that day. He told Ward that in the office. Ward said, "No you can't quit. We've got some busy times ahead and we need you." Kip said, "I quit." Ward got mad and said,

"You're not quitting" and pushed Kip. Kip (angry) said, "I quit" and punched Ward in the nose. Ward landed in the chair. Ward said to Kip, "You'll never work in Peddleton again." Two days later, Kip was working at a local pizza place.

During one of my days off in mid December, one of the toilets in the women's restroom was stopped up really bad. Cody and Walter Hickenbottle were trying to get it unstopped. Cody told Ward that they had plunged the toilet many times and still was stopped up bad. Ward told them to keep trying. Cody told me they tried for almost 45 minutes. Cody (angry) said to Ward, "Look, this toilet is really stopped up bad." Finally, Ward called someone from the store office and they came and fixed it.

1979-VARN

Chapter 4

1989

During the first week of January, I was on my break. Mark came in and said something to Tawney about there being some tiny rocks on the parking lot. Nina comes downstairs to tell me about it. I said, "I would sweep them up after I get off break." She said, "Mark wants you to do it now." I got mad and said, "That's a bunch of god damn bullshit. I'm so fucking tired of this god damn place."

About a week later, I was coming back in from sweeping the parking lot. I immediately noticed that the plastic strips were put up over the cooler door. Tawney comes up to me and says, "What are those strips doing up there?" I said, "I didn't know who put them there." She said, "Well, you're back here quite a bit aren't you?" I said, "Yeah, but I didn't put them there." She said, "If I find out you put those strips up there, you're going to pay for that food if it spoils." I (angry) said, "Oh no I'm not." If she would've said another word about those strips, I was going to cuss her out.

A week later, the basement flooded. Walter and I had to clean up the flood. That took a good hour and a half. Well, 12:30 PM had rolled around and the basement flooded again. This time, it was worse. Walter and I were supposed to get off at 1:00 PM. Instead, we got off at 4:00 PM.

The next day I was on break. I was taking my food downstairs. Swing manager John Balson was attempting to ring me up for my food. Swing manager Carla Dallion had already rung up my food. I told John I had already been rung up. He said, "Who rung you up?" I said, "Carla did." He then said, "Who rung you up?" I said, "Carla did." He again said, "Who rung you up?" I (angry) said, "Carla did." After that, I just walked away.

During mid February, someone on night shift mopped the lobby with grease. Guess who had to re-mop the lobby? You guessed it, I did.

During the first week of March, the store was out of glass cleaner. Ward was accusing Walter of not doing his job. Keith said something to me about the windows not being cleaned. I told him there was no glass cleaner. He said, "Use dish soap." I went and washed the windows. When I got finished, Ward said something to me about the windows not being cleaned. I told him there was no glass cleaner. He said, "Why didn't you say something?" I had mentioned there was no glass cleaner. I had also left a note in the office saying, "We need glass cleaner." Ward said, "There was no note." He said, "I'm going to put an ad in the newspaper that the Burger Store needs a janitor." He sounded like he was going to fire Walter. Ward then said, "I might put an ad in the newspaper that the Burger Store needs 2 janitors." He sounded like he was going to fire me. If he was to fire me, I would go on unemployment. The thing was, he had to chew me out in front of everybody. Ward wouldn't chew me out downstairs where nobody was around. I think he was afraid that I would kick his ass, and he wouldn't have any witnesses. A lot of times when we were out of a certain product, we would tell Ward. He always said, "I'll order it." When it didn't come in., he would say, "Why didn't you tell me?" A few minutes after Ward and I got into it, Ron Stolver made sarcastic comments about me not cleaning the windows. That really pissed me off. I said, "Hey look, I said I wasn't able to because there was no glass cleaner." If Ron had said another word about the windows, I was going to kick his fat ass.

In mid March, Cody quit the Burger Store. He was scheduled to work one Saturday but was scheduled to work at a local grocery store. He called and told them he couldn't work. LuAnn said, "We'll just have to fire you." Cody said, "No, I quit."

At the same time, the Burger Store hired Sherwood Chelburn as a janitor. Ward had him trained at the store in Long Branch. He didn't want Sherwood to be trained by Walter and me. After Sherwood worked a few days, my co-workers were complaining about him. They said he stunk. He sure did. I don't think he ever wore any deodorant. I remember on time

Jeanette was washing dishes. There were 3 basins in the kitchen sink. She said, "Greg, when you clean the filtering machine, you always keep the grease in one basin." She said, "Sherwood gets grease in all 3 basins." She was almost crying that day.

Also in mid March, I was getting this pan down from the cabinet for Fonda. Well, when I went to get it down, pickle juice splashed on the both of us. We were both extremely pissed. Ward opened that morning. Someone on night shift put that pan in the cabinet with pickle juice in it. It was also caked with grease. Ward found out about it and looked at the schedule to see who worked the night before. He said something to the night shift. It never happened again.

The complaints about Sherwood continued. My co-workers said that he was lazy. I remember one time in late March, Sherwood was going out to the freezer to bring in stock. He accidentally hit a customer's car in the drive-thru with the two-wheeler. It did some damage to the car. When Mark found out about it, he was not happy. The last Thursday in March, truck ran that day. Well, Sherwood decided to call in sick that day. LuAnn was trying to get him to come in to work. She was saying, "You can't call in, it's truck day." She wasn't able to get Sherwood to come in and work. I was supposed to get off at 9:00 AM that day. Instead, I had to work until 1:00 PM. That left me to do truck and the rest of the work by myself. The following Sunday, truck ran that day. I was scheduled to get off at 9:00 AM. Sherwood showed up that day and complained that he was sick. He wasn't sick. He just didn't want to work. We unloaded the dry stock and the cooler stock. When it came time to unload the freezer stock, Sherwood used that fake cough like he used the Sunday before. He said he couldn't do freezer stock. When I was unloading the freezer stock, Fred kept on saying, "Come on Sherwood, do something." When I was finished, Sherwood kept trying to switch schedules with me. I wouldn't do it. Sherwood kept saying he was sick and throwing up like crazy. Take my word for it, he wasn't sick. LuAnn asked me "Did Sherwood ask to trade schedules with you?" I said, "Yes he did." LuAnn was furious. She made Sherwood stay until 1:00 PM. Later that day, Fred was unloading stock at the Crestenview store. He was telling Paul Chelburn about Sherwood. Fred said, "You ought to see that asshole who's helping Greg at the Jedsen

Street store." Paul said, "Are you talking about my brother?" Fred said, "I'm sorry, I didn't know. I really didn't know." Paul said, "Hell, don't be sorry. Sherwood is the sorriest son of a bitch I've ever seen. He's lazy and won't do anything." I know it's bad when people say terrible things about you. When your own family says terrible things about you, it's even worse. Two days later, Sherwood quit. He no-showed that day. He was going to get fired but came in that morning and told Tawney he quit. She said, "OK, but please stay back." She said that because he stunk.

A few weeks later, both of the water nozzles were stolen. I kept them in a cabinet in the basement. The thing was, one worked and the other one didn't. People will steal anything.

A month later, Molly told me to put shake mix in the shake machine. I put a full bag in the machine. She said, "It still needs mix." So, I put in another full bag. It was totally full. Molly (angry) said, "We need shake mix." Mark was there and I showed him that the machine was full. He said there had to be something wrong with the machine. One of the lines was loose. Molly should not have talked to me the way she did.

The next day, the Burger Store had a picnic for all the employees. Tawney and Cheryl wanted me to fix them a plate of food. I said, "Get it yourself." I guess they thought I was their butler or something.

Two months later, I had scrubbed the drive-thru pad one morning. One hour later, Lyle comes in and tells me (from a distance) to scrub it again. That really pissed me off. As Lyle was walking to his car, I ran after him. I ran after him because I was going to kick his ass. As I was running after Lyle, LuAnn stops me and says, "Don't worry Greg, you don't have to scrub the drive-thru pad again." She said, "I saw you scrubbing it this morning."

During late July and early August, Kent Wervington, manager of the Crestenview store, filled in while Tawney was on vacation. He made everybody's life a living hell. He would make my co-workers triple stack food in the bin. It wasn't even that busy. The store had wasted a lot of food because of Kent's stupidity.

During the first weekend in August, there was a sign in the break room that said, "Certain employees were going to get paid vacations." Well, come to find out, the Burger Store was not going to do that. Jay was pissed and wrote "bullshit" on the sign. Someone had torn off the word "bullshit". Jay wrote "bullshit" on the sign again. The sign was taken down the next day. The next weekend, another sign appeared in the break room. This sign said, "Employees should bow down to their managers." I showed the sign to Jay. He wrote "fuck you" on it. The next day, the sign was taken down.

In early October, the Burger Store had a meeting. It was held at a church about a half mile away. Colleen Shellwater would not attend the meeting because it was in a church. Colleen was a devil worshipper. She had been known to drink blood. Lamar Bachtold and I said, "If she tries to drink our blood, she was going to have to fight us." Colleen quit a week later. However, at the meeting, Mark decided he would give employees who had been at the Burger Store a year or longer, a week's paid vacation.

In mid November, night swing manager Darby Ferk was making enemies left and right. Nobody liked him. Darby had his car egged just a few days before Thanksgiving. I never did find out who did it. A few days later, Darby was driving a brand new car. He had rich parents.

During the first week of December, Darby made yet another enemy. That enemy was Marilyn Kromes. Darby was making her do 10 things at one time. He was getting angry with her. Marilyn finally snapped. They were arguing in the office. She grabbed Darby and slung him in the chair and said, "Look mother fucker, don't you ever do that to me again." Darby goes and tells Ward about Marilyn. Darby begged Ward to suspend Marilyn for a week. Well, Darby got his wish. After the suspension, Marilyn quit.

During the second weekend of December, Arnold Pretz and I were out in the freezer getting stock. Some guy walks up to me. He asks, "Do you know of a place that is hiring a mechanic?" I said, "I don't know of any." He kept on asking me the same question. I said, "You need to look in the newspaper. You can also call some of the local garages." He continued to ask me the same question for about 10 minutes. I thought that guy would never leave. I guess he thought I was a newspaper. I wasn't black and white and read all over.

A few days later, Molly had been writing bad checks and signing Tawney's name to them. Molly got caught and was demoted to biscuit maker at the store in Long Branch.

1979-VARN

During mid December, Darby was going out with Trisha Balen. The thing was, Darby was gay. He was just trying to hide his homosexuality. About a week later, Trisha no-showed and Darby wrote her down as a no-show. Trisha found out about it and broke up with him.

A week before Christmas, Vern Doyce was fired after a week. He did his job. Ward fired him because he had a touch of green coloring in his hair. I think Vern was fired because he was black.

Chapter 5

1990

The Burger Store had an inspection coming up in late January. I was working quite a bit. Arnold quit January 23. I was the only janitor there. The Burger Store was going to hire some guy named Rob as a janitor, but he didn't show up for his interview. From January 25 to February 5, I worked 12 straight days. When the pay period ended January 31, I wound up with 110+ hours.

On February 6, I had a day off. It would be the only day I would have off all month. I worked 22 straight days starting February 7 to February 28. When the pay period ended February 15, I had 100+ hours. When the pay period ended February 28, I had 95 hours. I had been sent home early on 2 of those days because of so much overtime. One time during February, I had to do truck by myself. There was no one to slide the stock to me downstairs. I had to go back upstairs, catch the stock, slide it downstairs, catch it again, and stack it. That went on for 10 minutes. Then, Fonda finally helped me. Jay came in a few minutes later and helped me. During the third week of February, I was putting up stock downstairs. Jay came downstairs to tell me about this certain guy. This guy always wanted his biscuits fixed a certain way. Well, Jay came downstairs to tell me that guy farted. I said, "Yeah! What did it sound like?" Jay said, "It sounded like someone said, my herpes." At about the same time, Molly gets promoted back to swing manager.

When the first 2 days of March arrived, I had those days off. Man was I tired. From January 25 to February 28, I had worked 34 out of 35 days.

During the third weekend in March, Fred was running late. The area where Fred lived, had sleet the day before. He had a little trouble getting started. Fred would arrive at 4:45 AM. He was supposed to be there at 4:00 AM. When Fred arrived, Ward was bad mouthing him. Ward was saying, "I'm tired of getting my employees in here at 4:00 AM, and you show up late." Fred had explained that there was ice on the roads where he was. Ward, of course wouldn't listen. Ward didn't care if you were on your deathbed. He would still expect you to show up for work.

The store at Long Branch had a computer that ran messages like, "LARGE BURGER $1.95." Well, on the first Sunday in April, some of the employees typed in a message about Mel Cullingham. Mel was a swing manager at the Long Branch store. Mel was also gay. They typed the message just before the store opened. The message said, "MEL'S BLOW JOBS $1.95." Mel was off that day, but his mom and grandmother came in that morning. They saw the message. They were really pissed. They raised hell like there was no tomorrow.

During early April, Darby was complaining that dishes were not getting done fast enough. He said that dishes could be done in 30 minutes. The only way dishes could be done in 30 minutes is, if the person doing them was never interrupted. That never happened. The person washing dishes was always being called to help in the grill area or somewhere else. Darby finally got the message.

Another thing that happened in early April was Kyle Wollingford was needing an extra uniform. A note was left in the office saying, "Unless Kyle has permission to work naked, he needs a uniform." After I saw that note, I said, "If Kyle comes in here naked, I'm leaving." He wouldn't just scare the customers away, he would scare everybody else away.

During the second week of April, I was checking the men's restroom. I noticed someone was in the stall. All of a sudden, I heard that guy fart. Then, I heard him say (in a real spooky voice), "bastard fart." Then he said (in a real spooky voice), "I am the death of someone." After that, he said (in a real spooky voice), "I am going to get you." After he said that, I ran the hell out of there. I thought that guy might have been a devil worshipper. I told Jay what that guy had said. Jay said (with a little bit of anger), "That son of a bitch."

During the second week of April, new swing manager Carrie Houst had arrived. She was very rude. My co-workers and I immediately complained about her. In mid April, she made Abigail Bierce sweep and mop the lobby. Abigail was running the front drive-thru. Carrie was not supposed to do that. Well, when Tawney got back from the bank, she found out what Carrie did. Tawney was furious. Tawney jumped her case. Carrie would continue to make everybody miserable.

The day before Easter, Tawney transferred to the Burger Store at the Peddleton Mall. Having Tawney out of there was like a breath of fresh air.

In early May, Darby was pissing everybody off. Garrett had cleaned the floor around the dressing table. A few minutes later, Darby knocks a bunch of lettuce and onion scraps on the floor. He had also done the same thing to Jay and Ron. After Darby did his damage, Ron comes up to me and says, "Greg, how about let's Jay, Garrett, you and I gang up on Darby and whip his ass?" I said, "Great, when do we get started?" When Darby found out what we were going to do, he straightened up quickly. A few days later, Garrett and Fonda got into it over something. Garrett said something to her and she didn't like it. She then chased Garrett around the dressing table. She didn't catch him. We all had a good laugh over it.

In mid May, Thelma Winstern was supposed to get off at 4:00 PM. Her boyfriend was waiting on her. Instead, Darby made her stay over and do other things. She told Darby that her ride was waiting for her. Darby didn't care. It was 4:15 PM when Thelma got off work. Her ride had already left. However, her boyfriend returned 5 minutes later. Thelma's boyfriend went into the store and told Darby, "If you ever do that again, I'm going to whip your ass." Darby got the message and it never happened again. On May 25, the Burger Store on Fox Creek Road opened. Carrie was transferred there. Darby begged to be transferred there also. Darby got his wish. Everybody, along with myself, were glad to see them go. They were 2 of a kind.

This next episode did not take place at the Burger Store. Although, Jay and I were still employed there. Just a few days before Memorial Day, Jay and I had the day off. Jay came by my house and wanted to shoot the bull for a while. Jay asked me if he could make a prank phone call to Darby. I said, "OK." Jay called Darby (I was on the other phone listening).

Darby's mother answered. Jay asked, "Is Darby there?" She said, "No he's not." Jay said, "Well, he was supposed to give me a blow job." Darby's mother said, "Well, he didn't tell me anything about it." Jay and I just died laughing.

In mid June, the restrooms flooded. The drains had been stopped up. I put out of order signs on both restroom doors. Customers were still going into the restrooms. I was really pissed. It was obvious they couldn't read English. So, I put signs on both restroom doors that said, "Toillette ferme." That means, toilet closed in French. Surprisingly, those signs kept the customers out of the restrooms. It was obvious those customers could read French.

I was on vacation the second week of July. While I was away, I was told that Kyle went to the restroom to take a shit. The stall had no toilet paper. He forgot to check to see if there was any. Instead, Kyle went ahead and shit. Kyle wiped his ass with his hand. Swing manager Darrell Firley found out what Kyle did. Darrell asked Kyle, "Did you wash your hands?" Kyle said,

"Yeah." Kyle sounded like it was no big deal if he washed his hands or not. When I found out what Kyle did, I told my co-workers, "I'm never going in the store at night unless I know Kyle's not working." What Kyle did was very sick.

In September, Lita Bassenger noticed one of the pipes on the kitchen sink was leaking. Mark was in the store at the time. Lita showed Mark that the pipe was leaking. Mark said he would get somebody to fix it right away. Well, that leak didn't get fixed for a long time.

One day in early December, Garrett no-showed. That wasn't like Garrett to do that. I was supposed to be off the next day. Dena asked me if I could work tomorrow. She was afraid Garrett wouldn't show up. Ed Parver was scheduled to work janitor that day. I said, "What if Garrett shows up?" Dena said, "I'll let you off early sometime this week." As it turned out, Garrett did not no-show. He had called in sick the night before at midnight. Whoever took his call that night forgot to write down that Garrett had called in sick. Garrett showed up that day I was supposed to have off. I showed up that day for nothing. Did I get to go home early that week? "Hell no!"

Chapter 6

1991

In late January, Lita's daughter Teresa was having trouble with Nathan Tarmer. Nathan worked at the Burger Store but he was picking on Teresa at school. Lita wanted to get back at Nathan. She thought about putting cow shit in his jacket. He always hung his jacket in the break room. Lita thought since she knew that Nathan knew she had cows, Nathan would know it would be Lita that put it in his jacket. I told Lita, "Put your own shit in his jacket. He doesn't know what it smells like." A week later, Nathan stopped picking on Teresa.

The first Sunday in February, the store flooded. Ward blamed me for not cleaning the grease trap. I cleaned it once a week like I was told. The store had flooded on different occasions before, but I had always cleaned the grease trap when it needed to be cleaned. It was obvious that the grease trap wasn't the problem. Ward was saying things like, "When the bill comes from the sewer cleaning service, should I send it to your house?" I ignored him. If the bill was to come to my house, I would've put it back in the mailbox, just like Fred Sanford would do.

In mid March, Marcus Pilsen and I were working one morning, and the truck ran that day. Ward was the opening manager. Jim Barklam was the truck driver. Jim had a habit of being slow. He also had a habit of falling asleep right after I awakened him. Marcus and I woke Jim up twice. He had fallen asleep both times. Ward asked, "What is the hold up?" I told him that Marcus and I woke Jim up twice and he kept going back to sleep. Ward goes out to the truck and chews Jim out really bad. Jim said, "I took the rap for you." I thought, "What the hell are you talking about?" I didn't tell him to go back to sleep.

The second Monday in April, I was supposed to be off that day. Well, the day before, Dena asked me if I could work that Monday. She said that Katie Porlsan called in sick for that day. Katie worked front counter. I told Dena that Ed was scheduled to work that Monday. She said, "That might affect the schedule because Katie called in that day." Ed never worked front line. He always worked the janitor position or in the grill area. There was no way that would have affected the schedule. Well, I went in to work that day. Ed and I were both there. Ed was wondering what I was doing there. I told him what Dena did. Ed didn't understand it. LuAnn had opened that morning. I told her what had happened. She let me go home at 9:00 AM. She said, "That was stupid of Dena to do what she did." When I was leaving, Dena gave me a smirky look. I gave her an evil look right back. I was right and she knew it.

A month later, Ed and I smelled something that stunk. We said, "Something stinks around here." Emma Halsen sniffs her armpit and says, "Not me." Ed and I knew it was her that stunk. She must have gagged when she smelled her armpit.

A month after that, I was putting the chocolate ice cream container in the sundae machine. Ward had noticed a tiny bit of dirt on the lid. He got mad and said, "Don't you see that dirt on there?" The only way to see that dirt is to put your eye right on it. I think Ward was just mad because there was an inspection in a few days. I grabbed the lid and sprayed it off. Ward started saying things like, "You need to go look for another job." Then I heard him say, "I can't believe he didn't see that dirt on the lid." Ward was just blowing smoke. He didn't have the guts to fire me.

During the second week of June, the store had an inspection. Mark had treated the new inspector Corbin Brell to some golf and a few beers. I overheard them talking about it. Actually, what Mark did was kiss Corbin's ass. Mark knew if he treated Corbin to golf and beers, he would get good grades on the inspection. The store got 2 A's and a B. By the way, that pipe that was leaking 9 months earlier, finally got fixed the day before the inspection.

A few days after the inspection, Devon Freid forgot his work cap. Ward got him another one. Ward said, "Here, put that over your shit." Devon said, "At least I have shit to put it over." Ward didn't say anything to Devon. Ward didn't have much hair.

During the third Sunday in June, Mark told me to change the Coke tank. I went to change it. He says to change it again. He would tell me to change it 2 more times. He was pissing me off. Mark finally realized that there might be air in the line. A few months later, Cheryl came over from Long Branch to borrow a few things. She said to me, "Are you going to retire from here?" I said, "No." She said, "Yeah you are." I said, "No I'm not." She said, "Oh yeah you are." I (angry) said, "Oh no I'm not!" She didn't say anything after that.

In mid September, someone on night shift was pissing under the stairway in the basement. It went on for about a month. I thought, "What the hell do they think the restrooms are for?" Guess who had to clean it up? Yours truly.

The one thing that happened throughout that year was, that Dena screwed me out of time I was suppose to get off early. There would be times when was I at the dumpster throwing away trash. She would come out there and say, "I need you to stay later. There's word that the inspector may be stopping by the store." I had stuff I had to do on those days. Of course, I had to cancel my plans. The inspector never did stop by the store. That happened 6 times that year. Another thing that happened that year was Ward had the hots for Charlene Dooks. Although, she was going steady with Dylan Glevins. Ward even attended their wedding. The thing is, married couples were not supposed to work at the same store. Ward never allowed Ed and Dawn Parver to work at Jedsen Street. He made Dawn work at Long Branch. Ward did allow Dylan and Charlene to work at Jedsen Street.

Chapter 7

1992

In February, the store in Corlton had a problem with one of their frying vats. It was not heating. Phillip Wurd drove 45 miles to the Corlton store to see what the problem was. It turned out that they forgot to turn the switch from pilot to on after lighting the vat. Phillip made a trip for nothing. Also in February, Ward sent Wayne Kolmes to the freezer to get chocolate chip cookies. When Wayne came back in the store, he was carrying the container of cookies with one hand. The thing was, he was carrying the container on the palm of his hand over his head. When he got back in the store, he dropped the whole container of cookies on the floor. Lita and I said, "Oh my god." We were glad Ward didn't see what happened.

In early March, Garrett quit. He left no notice. Lita didn't find out until that morning. Ward came in and asked Lita why she was behind in work. Lita broke out crying. She said, "Garrett quit and I wasn't notified." Ward got the message and backed off.

On April 18, Ward worked his last day at the Jedsen Street store. Tawney returns as store manager. The employees had a going away get-together for Ward. He was going to be the store manager at the new store in Castle Bluff. It was also Dena's last day. She was also going to Castle Bluff. While I was at the get-together, I heard Dena say, "I can't believe Greg showed up." Dena had a bad habit of saying things behind my back. I had heard some of the things she had said. I always gave her an evil look and she turned away. The reason she had said what she said is, because Ward and I had our share of disagreements.

On April 20, the Jedsen Street store had a new swing manager. It was Chet Durcy. That same day, the Castle Bluff store had opened. Devon had gone in the Castle Bluff store the day it opened. He saw an employee taking out a big barrel of trash. Devon had seen Lyle there. Lyle said to that employee, "You be sure to bring that trash bag back, those things cost money." Devon thought, "You greedy son of a bitch." Devon told me about it. I felt the same way. Lyle had millions of dollars and he was worried about a stupid trash bag.

The moment Chet arrived, he was picking at everybody. Jay seemed to be his prime target. A few days after Chet arrived, he asked me to unhook the soda tank connectors and let them soak in hot water for an hour. I said, "There's no way I can do it now." It was 12:30 PM. That was a busy time of the day. The customers may want something to drink. I walked off after that. What Chet said made no sense.

During the first week of May, Jay was working one night and Chet was really picking at him. Jay told Chet, "Mark Grobe has always liked my work." Chet said, "That doesn't matter. It matters if I like your work." Jay got so pissed, he walked out. However, Jay was able to come back. At the same time, Devon was dating his co-worker, Ashley Poalen. Well, somehow Ashley's parents found out they were dating. Ashley's parents didn't like Devon.

They had to break up. Devon thought maybe Chet called Ashley's parents, and told them Devon was dating her. Devon said if he found out that Chet called her parents, Devon, along with Jay and Kyle were going to kick Chet's ass. I told Devon to count me in to kick Chet's ass also. I couldn't stand him. It was not Chet that called Ashley's parents. It was Devon's own cousin

Trina, that called. Ever since, Devon and Trina have not spoken.

A few days later, Tyrone Farger, a salaried manager had arrived at Jedsen Street. Shortly after he arrived, people were starting to complain about him. Shelly Verden definitely had problems with Tyrone. He was constantly picking at her. I found out that she had called him a nigger. I thought, "Uh-oh." I also found out that he had called her a bitch.

A month later, Tyrone asked Emma how to make a sunshine biscuit. Tyrone had been with the Burger Store for 5 years. When he asked how to make a sunshine biscuit, I knew something wasn't right about him. Tyrone should've known how to make one. He definitely didn't know how to do a truck order. We would be out of a certain item. He wouldn't order that item. We would have plenty of a certain item. He would order a whole lot more of that item.

During the first week of June, there was a problem with the women's restroom. Tara Fentrix went with me to see if anybody was in the restroom. Tara opened the door and the sound of a fart occurred. I said, "OK." I thought that was funny. During the second week of June, Chet was transferred to Fox Creek Road. We were all glad to see him go.

The Friday before Father's Day, Tyrone sent 6 people on break at 5:30 PM. Then at the same time, he was yelling at the few people he had working, to get with it. He was even yelling at the people he sent on break. You just don't send that many people on break at 5:30 PM. That is rush hour. People are getting off work. Tyrone pissed them off so bad that Shelly, Don Tilborn, Yolanda Klester, Bryan Parsten, Kyle, and LaFina Crozzle walked out. Somehow, Kyle was able to return. I found out that Tyrone had sexually harassed Yolanda and LaFina. They told Tawney about it but she did nothing about it. Tawney didn't seem to care. Yolanda and LaFina did file sexual harassment charges against Tyrone. I never did find out what happened though.

A few days later, Chet punched a young guy at Fox Creek Road. Chet did NOT get fired. He just got transferred to Castle Bluff.

During the third week of June, I took the American flag down because it started to rain. A few days later, some guy wrote in to the Talk Back section of the local newspaper. He said that I didn't show any pride to the flag. He said that I balled it up under my arm. That may have been true but I had to keep the flag from touching the ground. If Tawney had seen me let the flag touch the ground, she would have chewed me out for it. I made a comment to Talk Back about what that guy had said. He never said anything back to me.

A lot of things happened during the last week of June. One of them was, when Tawney asked me to turn off certain switches on the utility box. I told her I didn't know anything about that. I was never shown how to operate the utility box. We argued for about 15 minutes. Finally, I just gave up. I went downstairs and turned off some of the switches. That wound up being a mistake. I had shut things off that shouldn't have been shut off. Emma said something about me shutting off the grill. I said, "Don't start." I tried to tell Tawney that I didn't know anything about the utility box. You better believe that never happened again.

Another thing that happened was, Reggie McGaney was complaining about Ross not fixing things right. Reggie was complaining that one of the grills was not working properly. He said that he would not pay Ross 15 cents an hour. He would pay Ross $5 an hour to stay at home. Another thing was, when Tawney yelled at me because the water was left running at the hand washing sink. I did not leave it running. Keith heard what she did. Tawney apologized to me. It was a damn good thing.

The last thing that happened was at Fox Creek Road. Darby was going to make Jenny Waybern, carry a case of milk to the front counter. The case of milk weighed 35 pounds. Jenny was 7 months pregnant. She said she couldn't do it. Darby told her, "You better do it or it won't get done." Well, Jenny's husband Jake found out what happened. He told Darby, "If you ever do that to her again, I'm going to kick your ass."

In early July, Chet punched Wendy Reinfeld in the nose. Wendy's son, T. K. Wurley, was going to kick Chet's ass, but Ward told him not to do it. Ward said, "If Chet ever does that again, I will fire him." Chet should have been fired. He should have been fired, when he punched that guy at Fox Creek Road. The Burger Store was just hard up for employees.

During the last week of July, Darby stole $15,000 from the store safe. Mark found out about it. Darby was fired. Mark was going to have him prosecuted, but he told Darby, "Make sure you never work for the Burger Store ever again, or you will be prosecuted." I don't care if Mark had millions of dollars, $15,000 is quite a bit of money.

In late September, it was 12:45 PM. I was supposed to get off at 1:00 PM. Celia Broften comes up to me and says, "Tawney said for you to do dishes right now." That was not my job. Damn was I pissed. It was almost 2:00 PM before I got off work. I was so pissed off. When I got home, I grabbed my shirt and ripped it to shreds. It was OK. I had another shirt.

A few days later, Tyrone was transferred to Long Branch. He was suspected of drinking on the job. A few weeks later, he quit. A month and a week later, Tawney had me doing 10 things at once. Then, Keith comes in and tells Tawney that I need to do certain things. Tawney tells me, "Keith wants you to do the windows, urinals, and a bunch of other stuff." I got so angry and said, "I'm sick of this shit." Tawney said, "What did you say?" I just walked away. When 11:30 AM rolled around, Tawney sent me home. I asked her, "What about the stuff Keith wanted me to do?" She said, "Labor's high." I think she sent me home because of my attitude. I really didn't give a shit.

The Saturday after Thanksgiving, I was going about my work routine. All of a sudden, Keith comes in and wants me to do about 5 different things. A few minutes later, Lyle comes in and tells me to do about 10 other things. I was erupting into a purple face frenzy. There was no way I could've gotten all that stuff done by 1:00 PM. I didn't even get to go on break until 11:00 AM. Normally, I would take my break around 8:15 AM to 8:45 AM. I was so pissed that I told Celia, "I'm about ready to hurt somebody, so watch out." She didn't say a word. I got off break at 11:30 AM. When 11:45 rolled around, Tawney sent me home. I said, "What about all that stuff Keith and Lyle wanted me to do?" She said, "Do it some other time, labor's high." Well, just like earlier this month, I was probably sent home because of my attitude. But like I said before, I really didn't give a shit.

A week later, Wayne unloaded the truck, and a case of creamers was sent from the truck. The slide board wasn't even down. Wayne tossed the case of creamers down to the basement. The case hit the floor and creamers went everywhere. I'm glad I wasn't there when that happened. I'd like to know what he was thinking when he did that. On second thought, maybe it's best I didn't know.

1979-VARN

Chapter 8

1993

In early February, the Burger Store rehired Gaylon Willover. He had worked at the Burger Store, a few years ago. He was pissing everybody off. He would never do anything. I remember him saying, "If I owned the Burger Store, I would blow away the people I didn't like." Sandra Freid heard what Gaylon had said. She was scared to death. She told her husband about it. He said that Gaylon was probably just a lot of hot air. A few weeks later, Gaylon quit.

During the first week of March, the Burger Store was getting ready for inspection. Ned Falburt and Judd Waugsley were supposed to put up new shelves in the kitchen. The shelves were going to be put just above the dish washing sink. Ned and Judd were supposed to put the shelves up, a week before the inspection. They didn't put them up, until the very early morning, before the inspection. Lita said, "Ned and Judd almost got fired for not putting those shelves up when they were supposed to." I told Lita, "That was just a lot of hot air from Mark." He didn't want to get anyone else. The day before the inspection, Mark tried to treat the new inspector Tim Kooten to golf and a few beers. I found out that Tim didn't go for any ass kissing. The day of the inspection, Tim was giving everybody a hard time. Every time Tim would say something to Mark, all Mark would do was suck up to Tim. Mark wouldn't stand up for himself or his employees. The inspection did not go well.

A week after the inspection, the Burger Store hires Eli McBeil, as a salaried manager. He turns out to be not so smart.

1979-VARN

A real messed up day occurred on April 3. Preston Freid got fired that day. He was suspected of calling Tawney a whore. The thing was, he was suspected of calling her a whore on April 2. Preston did not work that day. Tawney had been asking everybody, if they heard Preston call her a whore. She had asked me if I heard him call her a whore. I said, "I don't know if he did, because I didn't work that day either." She asked Draylon Drice if he heard Preston call her a whore. He said, "Yeah." I think Draylon said what he did, because he didn't like Preston. Preston was fired because of hear-say. If Preston did call Tawney a whore, then she got what she deserved. I remember some years back, Tawney told me she had slept with a lot of different men. That whole day, Tawney treated me like shit. I was putting shake mix in the shake machine just before lunch time. Tawney tells me not to fill it past the full line. I (angry) said, "I know." She got mad and I walked off. A little later that day, Tawney had the nerve to say, "I've always treated you, the way you wanted to be treated, haven't I Greg?" I shook my head no. Then Tawney got smart and said, "Now Greg." I walked off again. When I shook my head no, some people were smirking at me. I didn't know what the hell their problem was. I was right and they knew it. I was telling people, "I am tired of working my god damn ass off, and still getting treated like shit." Ed and Celia came up to me and said, "We're sorry if we had treated you wrong." I said, "It wasn't you that was treating me wrong. It was Tawney." Tawney had caused me to go into a purple face frenzy that day. When I got off work, she about got mad because, it was time for me to get off work. I was so mad that, when I got home, I grabbed my shirt, and ripped it to shreds. My mom said, "I see you ripped up one of your shirts." I said, "Yeah! and I don't give a fucking damn."

A week later, Tawney and Celia had me doing a bunch of stuff. Well, Celia's brother, Tommy, noticed that Tawney and Celia had me doing a bunch of stuff. Well, Tommy told me to do something. I was pissed off, and was throwing a temper tantrum. Assistant manager Wade Seinford comes up to me and says, "What's going on?" I said, "I was a little upset at what Tommy told me to do." Wade said, "A little?" Then he said, "Forget it."

A week later, truck ran that day. I had to be at work at 3:45 AM. Well, Eli had closed the night before. Sometimes employees would not get out of there until 2:00 AM or 3:00 AM. Eli called me at 3:00 AM. He said that the truck was here. I said, "I know." He says, "Aren't you supposed to be here?" I said, "I don't have to be there until 3:45 AM." He asked me if I had a key to get in to the store. I said, "No I don't have a key." He said, "OK I'll let you in when you get here." After I hung up, I thought, "What a dumb ass." Only managers were allowed keys to the store. My mom got woke up by Eli's call. She asked me who it was. I told her, "It was damn Eli." It was a good thing my mom was getting up soon. Eli would've gotten cussed out. After I had put up stock that day, Devon played a joke on Wayne. Devon told him that he couldn't touch both of his ankles, and spell run 3 times. Well, Wayne touched both of his ankles and said, "RUN, RUN, RUN." So, Devon tells Wade about that joke he played on Wayne. Wade tells Wayne that he couldn't touch both of his ankles, and spell run 3 times. Wayne (again) touches both of his ankles and says, "RUN, RUN, RUN." Wayne never caught on to the joke. That same day around noon, I had heard that labor was high. Certain people were being sent home early, including me. Celia even sent Calvin Breckleburg home early. Calvin was scheduled to wash dishes. The dishes did not get done. The night shift got mad about it. Wade and I would have to do dishes the next morning. We were not happy about it at all. Later that day, our paychecks had arrived. Patty Kultz had called in sick that day. She came in to get her check. They wouldn't give it to her, because she called in sick.

A week later, some guy called me at 5:45 AM and said, "I made love to 12 men." I said, "Good for you." I never did find out who made that call. It was just somebody playing a prank.

A few days later, the bread truck had arrived. The truck driver's name was Moe Whacken. That day there was a different driver. When he walked in I said, "Is Moe Whacken off today?" The guy said, "Yes he is." I started laughing my ass off, after I realized what I said. It sounded just like "wacking off." Everybody was asking me what was so funny. I told them and everybody was laughing.

A few days after that, I had to go and get Brady Glayson, and bring him to the store. The reason why I had to do that was, because his wife had beat him up. I told Tawney, "I hope I get some gas money for this." She (sarcastically) said, "You will." I said to myself, "It's not my job to go and get battered husbands."

On the last day of April, Marlene Goalers called in sick. She even called in for Stacey Croyle that day. Stacey wasn't even scheduled to work.

One night during the first week of May, Kyle was messing things up. Wade was getting frustrated with him. Wade said, "Kyle, if you don't shape up, I'm going to grab your dick, and smack you upside your face with it." The next night, Kyle continued to mess things up worse. This time Wade said, "Kyle if you don't stop it, I'm going to suck your dick." I think Wade was so frustrated, he didn't know what he was saying. I couldn't help but laugh though.

A few months later, the Burger Store hires Rena Mogley to work front counter. A month later, she is promoted to swing manager.

In early October, Kyle got fired for sniffing the gas, out of a whip cream can. Frida Bassenger caught him. Tawney fired Kyle on the spot. Also in early October, Chet quit the Burger Store. Everybody was glad to see him leave. He gets engaged to former Long Branch swing manager Lachelle Morkers. When I found that out I thought, "Hard to believe there was a woman that desperate." I thought he might punch her.

During the second Saturday of October, it was really busy. Roy Carian was working his ass off. The thing was, everybody was picking at him. Roy got so angry he yelled, "I'm tired of this god damned mother fucking bullshit." Tawney got onto him for saying that. I'm surprised Roy didn't get fired. Roy was a real good worker. I didn't blame him for saying what he said.

A few days before Thanksgiving, the Burger Store hires Jill Kender to work front line. Shortly there after, customers and employees complained about her being rude.

About 2 weeks after Thanksgiving, I did not go on break until 11:00 AM. I had tried to go on break earlier, but Tawney was making me do everything and more. She got pissed off at me for going on break late. I got called off my break twice to help them out. I wound up having to get ice for the front counter. You talk about being pissed off. When I got through getting ice for the front counter, I went into a purple face frenzy. I went downstairs and ripped my shirt to shreds. It was OK, I had another shirt hanging in the break room.

A couple of things happened throughout the year. One of those things was about Wayne. Wayne was always dropping stuff. He wouldn't watch what he was doing. I remember on the second Sunday in December, the Burger Store had a bowling party. Wayne was getting a bowling ball, and dropped it. It missed my toe by an inch. Lita said, "He is such a klutz." Whenever Wayne would filter the grease, he wouldn't keep an eye on the draining funnel. The funnel would get clogged with fries. Grease would go all over the floor. The grease would sometimes flow up to the front counter area. Wayne would have a puddle of grease, the size of a lake. The other thing was that, Tawney used Celia and Allison Drice like puppets. Tawney had them do her dirty work. I remember Tawney saying to both of them something like, "Could you have Greg do that? He might get mad at me." I thought, "Scared huh?" Sometimes Allison would get Celia to have me do something. Allison was afraid I'd get mad at her. Allison was also scared sometimes.

Chapter 9

1994

In early February, Tim came by for a visit. He constantly complained about the store not being in satisfactory condition. Finally, Tawney (angry) told Tim, "My employees do the best they can." She said, "It was not easy to keep the store running the way it should." She also said, "If you can do a better job of running the store, then go ahead and try." For once, I liked what Tawney had said.

Later that month, I had to go to Fox Creek Road and help Monte Halixon unload truck. I had unloaded many trucks by myself. I guess they didn't want Monte to unload truck by himself.

On the first Saturday of March, Tawney quits the Burger Store. Lyle supposedly hit her on the butt. She had complained about it many times before, but this time, she had enough. Tawney did win some kind of settlement against Lyle. No one knows what kind of settlement she actually won. It was great not to have her as store manager anymore. Wade becomes store manager.

During the second week of March, the Burger Store got comment cards for the customers. Customers began commenting that the store needed to get rid of Jill. They said that she was rude. They were right. The store never got rid of her.

The third Saturday in March, Wayne was holding the freezer door open for me, so I could put up stock. Jill said that Wayne ought to close the door on me. Wayne said, "He wouldn't do that to a friend." Jill said, "Greg's not a friend, he's just there." I wasn't happy about what she had said. Jill did apologize for what she said. I didn't want her apology, so I walked away.

On the first Tuesday in April, the store got 20 phone calls in 5 minutes. It was about 9:30 AM to 9:35 AM when this happened. A lot of the calls were people asking, "Is the store open?" I thought, "How stupid are they?" I told my co-workers, "The store ought to get an unlisted number." Most of them thought that was funny. Gabe Pallons didn't think it was funny. He said, "This is a public place. It can't have an unlisted number." Gabe had no sense of humor. I was only kidding, he didn't have to take me serious.

During the later part of the first week of April, Carlton Jebbords threw a cup of Dr. Pepper at Lisa Gillard. The next day, Carlton asked Lisa for a date. Lisa, of course, turns him down. Carlton should have known that Lisa wouldn't go on a date with him, especially after what he did. A few days later, Carlton gets fired for swearing.

On the second Tuesday in April, Nora Bachtold walks out after 12 years of service. She finally had enough of the Burger Store. She was upset because she was not getting paid enough an hour.

A few days later, Jesse Bolders and I were unloading truck. Jill had opened that morning. While Jesse and I were unloading truck, Jill walks by and says, "Good looking red head coming through." I said to Jesse, "I didn't see Reba McEntire coming through here." Truck driver Gary Kreely said, "I didn't see my wife come through here either." Jesse asked me, "What would you do if Jill was sent out of the truck naked?" I said, "Send her back and stamp "reject" on her."

During the first week of May, I had to go Castle Bluff, and get sundae and shake mix. It was 17 miles to Castle Bluff. Mark said, "There was no other stores closer to loan us mix." Mark wouldn't even send one of the maintenance guys from the office, to pick up the mix. Those guys had trucks. He just had to send me. I could barely get the mix in my car. Mark only paid me $5 as gas money. Also during the first week of May, Mark was going to buy a new ice machine. He told Ross, Judd, Phillip, and Ray Trouse, not to order any parts for the ice machine. What does Ross do? He orders new parts. Mark told him not to do it. Mark did not buy a new ice machine. He told Ross to try the new parts, and see if they would help. The ice machine would continue to mess up many times.

It was a little over a year since Brady's wife had beat him up. This time, Brady beat up his wife. She filed charges against him. He also filed charges for when she beat him up. The court dismissed both cases. Brady and his wife made up for their differences. Although, all of this didn't happen at the Burger Store, Brady was employed there, when all of this happened. By the way, Brady and his wife now have 2 kids.

In mid May, Wayne dropped a burger on the floor. He picks it up, and tries to use it. He tells me to keep quiet. Lita sees him from a distance. She makes Wayne throw the burger away. A day later, Donnie Balger drops chicken nuggets on the floor. He attempts to put them in a 12 piece box. Well, a 6' 4" 260 or so pound guy, at the front counter, had ordered a 12 piece chicken nugget. That guy saw Donnie drop the nuggets on the floor. Donnie put them in a 12 piece box. The guy complained right away. I mean he was furious. Wade made Donnie throw the dropped nuggets away. Donnie quit the next day. Donnie went to work at a local pizza place. He would do deliveries only. They didn't want him handling food. They found out what he did at the Burger Store.

On May 31, the Burger Store loses 3 employees. Keith quits. He opens 3 fast food shops of his own. Ward becomes supervisor. Jill quits. We, along with the customers, are glad of that. Ray also quits that day. Ross was put in charge of maintenance. I always thought Ray was a fairly good worker. I remember Ray said, "I was always working my ass off. Ross would sit on his ass and do nothing." Ray told Mark, "I'm sick of the bullshit."

The ice machine broke down on the fourth Sunday of July. Lita called Ross at 5:30 AM to fix it. Ross would not come and fix the ice machine. Lita was pissed. She then calls Mark's house. Mark's wife, Annette, answers the phone. Annette says, "What's wrong Lita?" She says, "Ross won't come and fix the ice machine." Annette then calls Lyle. Lyle calls Lita and says, "What's the problem Lita?" She said, "Ross won't fix the ice machine." Lyle said, "Take some money out of the safe. Get you about 10 bags of ice or however many you need, and I'll take it out of that bastard's paycheck. Just because he's married to Sally, doesn't mean he's going to pull that kind of shit." Well, Ross did come by about 8:00 AM. He stood against the ice machine with his face down. He was standing against the ice machine, as if he was being searched by a police officer. He stood like that for 3 minutes, and left the store. Ross didn't even get fired. If I would have done what Ross did, I would have gotten fired.

About 5 days later, Devon was talking to Brady at the store. Tana McGaney got onto Devon for talking to Brady. Devon said, "All I did was ask him, what was on a deluxe chicken sandwich." Well, the next morning I came into work. Devon told me what happened. He told me, "Tell Tana, she's a whore." I wasn't going to tell her that. Tana and I always got along. Devon told his dad about what happened. His dad called the Burger Store home office. Tana was transferred to Long Branch a few days later.

In early September, Devon returns to the Burger Store, after a year and a half absence. Mark sees him at another fast food place. Mark tells him that, Tawney was no longer there. Wade was the store manager. Devon never did get along with Tawney. I think that was the reason Devon returned, since Tawney wasn't there. The moment Devon came back, he would act all crazy. Whenever we unloaded truck, he would put wrestling moves on boxes. Devon would say, "Hulk Hogan, off the ropes, boot to the head." He would also say ,"Lex Luger, running forearm." I remember one time, Devon power bombed an empty shortening container 6 times. After the 6th time, he said, "Get up boy." He would even grab something that resembled a microphone, and would sing into that object, especially Motorhead songs. Also, whenever the truck driver would throw plastic wrapping off the truck, Devon would wad the plastic wrapping up, and drop back to pass. He would pass the plastic wrapping to himself. Then, he would run about 40 yards and say, "Touchdown." Then he would spike the plastic wrapping. He would sometimes take Lita's hand, and start dancing with her. While he was dancing with Lita, he would sing "Strangers In The Night." Devon had me laughing so hard, I practically had tears in my eyes. There was never a dull moment, when Devon was around.

During the first Saturday in October, I was washing windows. We were really busy that day. I saw a guy walk in the store. Well, about 5 minutes later, that same guy walks out and says to me, "They got you washing windows, and I can't even get waited on in there." I was just doing my job. Then, the woman that was with that guy said, "You can't even get waited on in there?" He said, "Hell no, they're even slower than you." It sounded like, she needed to find her another man.

Paychecks arrived on November 2. Robby Geel called in that day because his leg was hurting. A few hours later, he comes hobbling in the store to get his check. One of the managers gave him his check. Devon and I thought that Robby shouldn't have got his check, since he called in that day.

The Burger Store rehires Jolene Aubern a few days later. She had worked at the store, back in 1991. She had gotten fired for not taking a bath or shower. She stunk all the time. Jolene was also lazy. Whenever Jolene opened front counter, she would never bring up any cups, or anything else from the stockroom. The other front counter employees complained. Jolene always said she stocked the front counter, but she never did. Jolene also had a bad habit of grabbing my shirt, especially when she was asking me a question. The first time she grabbed my shirt, I let it slide. The second time, I told her not to do that anymore. The third time, I got so mad, I elbowed her. She didn't do anything about it. It was a damn good thing.

About 5 days after Thanksgiving, Floyd from Crestenview, came by to get 14 cases of regular burgers. About 20 minutes later, Kent comes to get about 8 cases of big burgers. Kent asked me, "Did Floyd come by to get the regular burgers?" I told him he did. He wouldn't take my word for it. He even asked Wade and Lita, but he wouldn't take their word either. We even showed Kent the paper that Floyd signed, when he picked up the burgers. Kent didn't believe it. He had to call Crestenview to see if Floyd picked up the burgers. I thought, "You asshole."

A week later, I was just coming in at 7:00 AM. Devon was complaining about Wayne spilling grease on the floor. Devon was really pissed about it. The first thing Devon said to me was, "Wayne spilled grease on the floor. I'm not cleaning it up, and you're not cleaning it up either." I wasn't going to clean it up anyway. Wayne finally cleaned it up at 7:45 AM.

The second Friday in December, Tim was there for a visit. Wade had Devon and I go up on the roof, and find a place to put Christmas lights. A few minutes later, Devon saw a flagpole and says, "uh-oh! uhhh-oooh!" He goes up to the flagpole, and starts singing a Motorhead song. I about busted a gut laughing. Wade changed his mind about the Christmas lights. We went up there for nothing. It was really funny seeing Devon imitate Lemmy Kilmister of Motorhead. After all, we did get to bullshit for 20 minutes.

A few days later, Wade sent Devon to the store at the plaza, to unload truck. The plaza didn't have anybody to unload truck. Well, when he got to the plaza, Devon and supervisor Doby Dallons got to talking about music. Devon told Doby, "I like KISS." Doby said, "They made millions by wearing make-up." Devon said, "That's the American way." Devon and Doby continued to argue about KISS. Devon said to Doby, "You're a bald headed bastard." Cheryl comes along and tells Devon, "You've got 30 minutes to put up stock." Devon said, "I'll take as long as I like." That was the last time Devon would unload truck at the plaza. Cheryl did not like his attitude. The next time the plaza had a truck, Wade sent me to unload it. I went to the plaza. Doby and I got to talking. He said he had heard of me. I told him I had been at the Burger Store for 9 years too long. He said "No you haven't." I said, "Oh yes I have." He said, "No you haven't." I (angry) said, "Oh yes I have!" He said nothing else. By the way, KISS is my favorite rock and roll band.

Chapter 10

1995

During the first week of January, Long Branch was needing a janitor. Wade said that Harriet Altenbach, a swing manager at Long Branch, was kind of rough on janitors. Devon said (anxiously), "Send me over, send me over." Wade decided not to, because he was afraid Devon would cuss her out. Devon was capable of doing it.

On the second Friday in January, Judd and Ned sat out in the lobby for 4 hours. All they did was talk, drink coffee, and smoke cigarettes. I know they should have been doing their work. Devon was really pissed about that. Mark had stopped by that day. Devon said to Mark, "Why is it that Greg and I work like dogs, and Judd and Ned sit out in the lobby for 4 hours?" Mark said, "I will take care of that." Mark just said that to get Devon off his back. When Judd and Ned got through sitting in the lobby, they went in the kitchen. They replaced 2 wall tiles. That took a little less than 5 minutes. They left after that. They didn't even clean up their mess. Devon had to do that. He was not at all happy about it. If Devon and I, would have done what Judd and Ned did, we would have been fired.

On the third Saturday of January, Sandra was taking care of an incorrect order. Ward saw what was happening. He goes over to Sandra, and starts chewing her out. Sandra didn't even take that customer's order. Sandra was taking care of the mistake. Ward continued to yell at her. The customer said that Sandra was not at fault. That customer was standing up for her. However, Ward continued to yell at her. Sandra started crying. Well, Devon found out what Ward did. Boy was he pissed. Devon walked up to Ward and said, "Look Ward, job or no job, if you ever make my mom cry again, I'm going to break every fucking bone in your body." Ward did nothing to Devon. Ward did apologize to Sandra. It was a good thing.

A few days later, Jolene quit. She was about to get fired. She would not take a shower or bath. I was glad to see her go. That was one thing Ward and I agreed on, we didn't like Jolene.

On the last Sunday in January, Devon was training Sal Alsted, to do janitor work. They had just got through cleaning the filtering machine. Wayne decides to toss his time card in the air, and catch it. He caught it the first time. The second time, he dropped it in the French fry grease. Lita tells Devon what happened. Devon (angry) said, "I'm going to kill that bastard." Devon confronts Wayne. Devon said, "What the hell did you do that for?" Wayne said his card slipped out of his hand. The time cards were made from a chemical that was poisonous. If someone was to swallow the chemical, it would kill him or her. Devon and Sal had to change the grease. Devon quits 4 days later.

A month and a half later, Rhonda Feckner, manager at Fox Creek Road, comes over and starts bossing everybody around. The store was running fine. Wade was off that day. Assistant manager Heidi Geibert had everything under control. Rhonda was telling me what to do. I wasn't listening to her. I told Heidi, "I don't know who the hell she thinks she is, telling everybody what to do." Heidi said, "Try to keep cool." A few minutes later, Rhonda left. It was a damn good thing.

On the first day of April, the store had no lobby worker. I was doing dishes that day. Ward has me taking care of the lobby, and doing dishes at the same time. He got mad and said, "You need to take care of the lobby. The customers don't care if the dishes, get washed or not." I had changed all the trash in the lobby. The trash was really piling up in the back room area. The large trash can was overflowing. There was no room to walk, in the back room area. I took all the trash to the dumpster. Well, Ward comes outside looking for me. I was coming back from the dumpster. Ward walks towards me, and just looks at me. If he had opened his mouth, I was going to kick his ass. The next day, Devon returns to the Burger Store.

About 5 days later, truck ran that Friday. Wayne called in sick that day. He was the kitchen opener. Tara called in sick that day also. That was the third straight Friday, she had called in sick. I'm sure if she needed

Fridays off, they could arrange it. As soon as Devon and I, were through unloading freezer stock, Devon was called into the kitchen. I was left to do truck and janitor work, by myself. When 7:00 AM rolled around, the plaza called. Cheryl wanted me to unload their truck. I said, "No." Wade asked me, "Will you unload plaza's truck?" I said, "No." Lita and Sandra took my side on that issue. They thought, "Who was going to put up stock at our store? Who was going to do the janitor work at our store?" A few minutes later, Rhonda called. She wanted me to unload her truck. Wade told her, "I can't get him to unload plaza's truck. I know he won't unload your truck." As I was going on break, Wade comes up to me and says, "I don't know what's with your attitude lately. Why won't you unload plaza's truck?" I said, "Because this store needs me, to put up our truck, and do the janitor work." I told him, "I was just thinking of us." Wade realized the situation and forgot about it.

A few days later, Sonja Woggins would not eat in the break room with Wayne. Wayne would eat hot dogs every single day. She said "I'm tired of Wayne and his hot dogs." Sonja ate in the lobby instead.

A week after that, Wayne was getting eggs. He put the eggs on the cart. He used the cart to haul food to the kitchen. Wayne turned the cart over on its side. About a half a case broke. Wayne said (in a whiny voice), "I don't have time to clean it up." Well, guess who had to clean up those eggs? You got it. I did. I went into a purple face frenzy and said, "April 14, 1995 is the last time I clean up any of Wayne's messes." I told my best friend, Steve Ribbleton, about what Wayne did at work that day. Steve said, "Why don't they fire him?" I told him, "That will never happen, because Wayne always shows up for work." I told Steve many times, that Wayne was always making messes.

During the third week of April, Barry Darf transfers from Fox Creek Road. He immediately gets on everyone's nerves. A few days later, front counter worker Nicole Binner said, "Down a fish sandwich." Barry said, "Kiss my ass." I thought, "You idiot." Barry had been saying that Rhonda, was going to make him, a swing manager. Brock Wurden said, "If Barry was going to be a swing manager, I know I could be a store manager." All Barry knew how to do, was run his mouth.

1979-VARN

In early May, Lisa was having trouble with Ward. He was constantly jumping her case. Lisa was a good worker. Lisa said, "If Ward ever makes me really mad, I'm going to chop off his balls. Then, I'm going to wear them around my neck as a prize." I said, "Damn!"

The Burger Store hires Purnell Kead and Marisa Bewk in early May. All they do is get in the way.

Barry continued to piss everybody off. I remember one time, Barry pushed Sandra. Sandra said, "Don't push me." Barry said, "I'll push you if I want." Sandra said, "You may think you're tough, but my son Johnny, would tear you up." Barry said, "I don't care how tough Johnny is, as long as I can kick him in the nuts." I told Devon that Barry had pushed his mom. Devon gave Barry an ass chewing. Barry never did bother Sandra again.

During May, drawers of money kept coming up short. Those shortages led to the demotion of Wade, as store manager. It was sad because Wade was a good manager. He wanted to do a lot for his workers. Mark and Ward wouldn't let him. Carl Geibert became store manager. Carl was a good manager. I had worked with him many times. However, I felt that Wade was done wrong by Mark and Ward. Wade was demoted to assistant manager and transferred to Castle Bluff.

The pipe that had been leaking since 1986, finally got fixed. Mark decided he would finally buy a new pipe. I thought, "What the hell took you so long?"

Carl and Ward were not getting along. Carl talks to Mark about having a different supervisor. Doby Dallons becomes the new supervisor.

During May, Marisa was pushing the mop bucket twice. She turns the mop bucket over twice. Water goes all over the floor. Guess who had to help clean it up? You guessed it. I did. Marisa was always bumping into everybody. She was always making Devon mad. One time Devon said, "Marisa is going to be the death of me."

During the last week of May, Barry and I had a slight disagreement about something. He said, "You prick." I said, "You are." Barry did nothing about it. It was a damn good thing. A day later, Barry held a box cutter to Byron Crusten's throat. Nothing was done about it. I told Byron, "I would've knocked the shit out of Barry." Byron said that Barry didn't have the guts to cut him.

In early June, I took off for 4 days. Barry had been bragging that he could do janitorial work. I told him "There was more to janitorial work than filtering grease and bringing in stock." Barry worked those 4 days. When I got back, he got mad at me because of what he went through. He said, "I'm going to kill you." I ignored him. Barry was just a bunch of hot air.

During mid June, the Burger Store hires Daphne Crost. She had been fired from 3 fast food places for no-showing all the time. She was also not very friendly. When I found out about Daphne, I thought, "This place will hire anybody."

Also in mid June, the store flooded around 7:30 PM. One of the pipes had busted. The flood was so bad, the customers were complaining about the smell. Night manager, Clara Coffren, called Ross to fix the pipe. He fixed it, but 20 minutes later, the pipe busted again. Water was going everywhere. A few minutes later, Mark comes through the drive-thru. Clara tells Mark that the store is flooded. He said to call Ross. She said, "Ross fixed the pipe, but it busted again." He said, "Call Ross." Mark didn't even come in and see if there was any possible damage. All he cared about was getting his wife a chocolate sundae. Whatever respect I had for Mark, I lost it that day. LeRon Drouse was so pissed about the flood, he walked out. However, Doby allowed him to return. Doby didn't blame him for being disgusted at what happened. I know that Mark was probably laughing about the flood. If the health department or Tim Kooten would've stopped by, when the flood occurred, he would not have been laughing. They would have shut him down faster than you could count to one. However, Ross did fix that busted pipe. The flood also got cleaned up. That was one hell of a night.

During the third week of June, Wayne had opened one morning. Sandra was getting pissed. I heard her say, "Oh! This is so ridiculous." I said, "What's the matter Sandra?" She said, "It's 6:25 AM and Wayne doesn't have any food in the bin." I said, "What the hell has he been doing?" She said, "I don't know, but I'm getting tired of it." Tad McGaney was the opening manager. He had to stop working on his paper work, and help Wayne get food in the bin. Wayne was known for not having food in the bin, when it was time to open. Well, Lita found out what happened.

The next day, she made sure Wayne had enough food in the bin, when it was time to open. Boy did he ever.

A few days later, Harriet transfers from Long Branch. She transfers because she wasn't getting along with Cheryl. During a month's time, 20 people quit because of Harriet's big mouth. When she first arrived, employees and customers start complaining about her. The one thing that happened when Harriet first arrived was, the opening employees got one of their 10 minute breaks, taken away from them. We were to be at work at 4:30 AM. Harriet would sometimes be the opening manager. She complained that she could not make it there at 4:30 AM. What we did though was, take our first 10 minute break, but not clock out for it.

During June, Devon was working at Fox Creek Road. In no time at all, Devon and Rhonda were not getting along. Devon got mad at her and said, "Have you ever tasted Judd's cock?" She said, "I don't know what you're talking about." Devon said, "Don't lie to me, I can see the stretch marks a mile away."

On the last Sunday in June, the truck ran. Devon was not told that truck ran that day. While Devon was unloading truck, the bread truck arrives. Joni Versong, the swing manager, starts getting onto Devon, for not being able to keep up with what was happening. Devon said, "I wasn't told that the truck ran today." Joni cops an attitude with Devon. She said, "I'm telling Rhonda about your attitude." Devon says, "Tell God, see if I care." Joni says, "You can just go home." Devon said, "OK, I will." Devon whips his time card through the time clock and leaves. Devon said that he left a mess for them. He said that hardly anything got done. A few days later, Devon quit.

Another thing that Harriet would do was, she would put 10 to 20 creamers in her coffee. One time, Anna Holten asked her, "Would you like some coffee with that creamer?" Harriet got mad. Harriet was also very fat. It seemed like she weighed about 700 pounds.

In early July, Todd Stoges gets hired as a janitor. He turns out to be a fairly good worker. The only thing was, Harriet always jumped his case.

During the third week of July, Barry quits. We were all glad to see him go.

Two months later, Carl fires Daphne. She had no-showed a few days. Carl said that he got tired of it. Also, Marisa simply walks out, while on the clock. The next day, she asked for her job back. Carl said, "No."

During the first day of October, Purnell ran and yanked, the display off the drive-thru menu board. Harriet tells me to put it back, on the menu board. I said, "Purnell yanked it off." Purnell said, "The wind blew it off." The wind wasn't blowing that day. I had to put the display, back on the menu board. I was pissed. After I was finished, I told a few of my co-workers, what Purnell did. I told them, "If Purnell pisses me off one more time, I'm going to rip his damn head off and go bowling with it."

Harriet continued to get on everyone's nerves. In early October, Sonja and Harriet got into it over something. They were both swing managers. Sonja was the opening manager that day. Harriet came in at 7:00 AM. Harriet said something to Sonja. I don't know what was said. It made Sonja mad enough to leave at 7:15 AM. Sonja said that she just couldn't work with Harriet. It seemed like every time Harriet went into the kitchen, she would mess everything up. She didn't know what the hell she was doing. Harriet was definitely not smart. I remember one time, I had just got done filtering the frying vats. Harriet asked me 3 times, if I had filtered the vats. After the third time, I got angry and said, "Yes." She gave me the OK sign. I thought, "Damn! She needs a hearing aid."

During the second week of November, Harriet gets robbed, while making a deposit, at a local bank. She would work the next day. I asked her if she was alright. She said, "Yeah." To make matters worse, Lyle shows up that day and teased Harriet. He pointed his finger at Harriet (pretending he has a gun) and says, "Bang!" I thought, "You bastard." I know that I didn't like Harriet, but I would never wish anything bad on her. A week later, Will Stround asked me about Harriet getting robbed. He asked me, "What kind of car has she been driving?" I told him, "A gold Chevette." He said that he saw her driving a Porsche. Will also said that, he saw Harriet at a department store buying a big screen TV. He didn't think she got robbed. He thought that she pocketed the money. I think Will said those things because, he didn't like Harriet. Will worked with her for a couple of years, at Long Branch. I didn't believe Will. He was a big time liar.

A few days after Thanksgiving, this woman was walking near the store. She was talking to herself. It was like she was talking to an imaginary person. I remember her saying, "Don't you lay a hand on me, I'll knock the shit out of you." I thought, "That woman's crazy."

The Sunday before Christmas, I was sweeping around the back of the store. A car comes through the drive-thru. This guy sitting in the back seat of that car, starts bitching at me, about his order. I told him, "You need to speak to the manager." That guy got to the drive-thru window, and started yelling at Vanessa Werkfield. Vanessa tells Carl about that guy. Carl said that he would correct his order. That guy said, "I used to work at the Burger Store." Carl said, "Ah! bullshit." The guy got his order taken care of, and he was gone. I told Carl, "I had your back, if that guy was going to try anything."

On New Year's Eve, Devon stopped in to say hi to Sal. Harriet thought Devon worked at the Burger Store. Harriet said to Devon, "If you work here, then clock in." Devon said, "Fuck you bitch, I don't work here."

Chapter 11

1996

On the first Sunday in January, Harriet asked me to go count chicken nuggets and chicken patties. I counted both the nuggets and patties. I told her, "There were 14 cases of each." Harriet said, "14 of what?" I (angry) said, "14 nuggets and 14 patties." Harriet didn't say anything back to me. I told everybody, "I'm getting tired of Harriet and her stupidity." Everyone felt the same way.

About 2 weeks later, Harriet got mad about something. I had no idea what it was. Apparently, she thought it was my fault. She said, "I'm going to beat you up." I told my co-workers, "I don't know how she was going to do that. It takes her a week and a half to get downstairs."

On the first day of February, Marcy Joyce Pallinger gets promoted to swing manager. The moment she got promoted, the only thing she knew how to do, was run her mouth.

A few days later, I had to change the trash in the lobby. I was changing this one trash can. There were these guys who looked over at me. They noticed that trash can, did not have a bag in it. As I was taking a bag of trash, back to the big trash can. Those guys dumped their trash, into that trash can, that didn't have a bag in it. I got so mad, I showed my ass. Lita says, "Don't worry, I'll take care of it." I know she was mad because I showed my ass. I had every right to be mad. Those guys could have used another trash can. I told Carl what happened. He told me not to worry about it.

On the last day of March, Purnell was putting trash in the big trash can. Well, the lid got stuck underneath his chin. When Purnell tried to break loose, he flipped in the air, and landed in the trash can. I wasn't there when that happened, but Todd told me about it. I thought, "Damn, I wished I could've seen that."

During April, Myrna Froybert had been calling in sick a lot. She called in 2 straight days. She called in more times in 2 days, than I had in 10 ½ years. Myrna continued to call in sick. Finally, during the last week of April, Carl had seen enough. He told Myrna, "Either get well or quit." She was trying to get fired, so she could get unemployment. Carl knew what she had in mind. He would not give her an inch. Myrna realized that Carl wasn't going to fire her, so she quit.

On the last Sunday in April, former swing manager Bobby Welfton stops by, and gets a morning burrito. He takes one bite and nearly throws up. Wayne had saved left over burritos from the following day. He decided to serve one of them. It was the Burger Store's policy to throw away food, when breakfast was over. Lita found out what happened. She gives Wayne a "what for?" Wayne never did that again.

During the first week of May, Purnell nearly flips into the big trash can again. This time he saves himself. I told Carl, "Purnell nearly flipped into the trash can again." Carl said, "The next time Purnell lands in the trash can, roll him out to the dumpster, and throw him in there." I said, "OK."

A week later, the Burger Store hires Tori Jederson. She had worked at Long Branch, for a couple of years. She also spent time in jail for selling drugs. Like I said before, the Burger Store will hire anybody. Tori and I never agreed on anything. The only thing we agreed on was, that we didn't agree on anything.

During the third week of May, I was cleaning the men's restroom. Suddenly, a boy walks into the stall. All of a sudden, the boys mother yells, "Jared!" He says, "What!" The mother says, "Hurry up and get out of there." Jared says, "I'm using the bathroom." The mother says, "Well, hurry up." A few seconds later, the mother says, "Jared, get your ass out of there." Jared says, "Mom, I'm pooping." The mother says, "Jared, you better get out of there right now, or I'm going to bust your ass." Jared had to get up from the toilet. I thought, "You no good hateful bitch." I mean the boy hardly had enough time, for the shit to come out of his ass. He didn't even have time, to flush the toilet. I was afraid his mother would rush into the restroom. I went into the stall, after the boy had left. There was only 1 piece of paper in the toilet. He definitely didn't have time to wipe his ass. I felt sorry for that boy.

On the last day of May, Wayne was scheduled to work 9:00 AM to 5:00 PM. Tad was scheduled to work 6:00 AM to 2:00 PM. Wayne asked Tad, "Could you trade shifts with me?" Tad asked, "Why?" Wayne said, "Because there's a cartoon on at 3:00 PM, that I want to see." I thought, "Wayne, aren't you ever going to grow up?" If nothing else, Wayne could've set his VCR. Tad wound up trading shifts with him. Wayne begged him constantly.

In early June, Harriet gets put on night shift. People on day shift complained about her too much. At the same time, the Burger Store hires Will Stround. He came in thinking it was going to be like Long Branch. Will had to realize that, all Burger Stores were not the same. People also complained that Will was lazy. Marcy Joyce continued to run her mouth. She would always interrupt my important work, to do some stupid stuff.

During the second week of June, Wayne was carrying ice to the front counter. He always carried it on the palm of his hand, like a waiter. That day, Wayne dropped the bucket of ice. Ice went everywhere. A few customers were hit by ice cubes. They complained immediately. Lita started singing "Macho, Macho Man" to Wayne. He was always trying to be macho. Instead, he just made things worse for everybody.

In early August, the Burger Store hires swing manager, Simon Broast. He had worked at Long Branch and Crestenview previously. Lita immediately complains about him. She said that he didn't know what he was doing. I remember once, Simon and I were on break. He said that he didn't like Ward. He thought Ward was a smart ass. Simon said that he got along better with Doby. I told Simon, "Doby was always telling me how to do my job." Simon said, "Well, he should tell you how to do your job." I said, "Look, I've been here 11 years, I know how to do my job." Simon got up and left. I was right, and he knew it.

In mid August, I was unloading the truck. I picked up a case of potatoes, and hurt my back. My back hurt like never before. I told Harriet that I hurt my back. Harriet said, "It was nothing serious." I told her, "I need to go to the hospital." She said that I didn't need to go to the hospital. I told her, "My back is really hurting." Finally, after arguing with Harriet for 10 minutes, she let me go to the hospital. Luckily, all I had, was a slight pull of the lumbar. It was nothing serious.

During the first week of September, Harriet gets moved back to day shift. People had complained about her on night shift. I overheard a customer say to Harriet, "I thought you worked nights?" Harriet said, "I did, but I messed up."

On September 30, Wade quits after 15 years. Ward asked him to work, the first few days in October. Wade says, "No." Wade got a better job. Wade told me he was going to set his work shoes on fire. That same day, I came in to unload truck. I was not scheduled to work that day. Carl told me to put up stock and leave. Will was scheduled to work that day also. Will asked me if I would stay until 1:00 PM. Will was scheduled to work until 1:00 PM. I told him that I wanted to get off early. Will said, "I'm leaving at 6:00 AM, no matter what anybody says." Well, 6:00 AM rolled around, and Will left. He left early, because Carl was coming in at 7:00 AM. Carl would have definitely made Will stay until 1:00 PM. I told Carl what happened. He said, "Filter the frying vats, and bring in stock for lunch. You can go after that." I wound up leaving at 9:00 AM. Exactly 2 weeks later, Will leaves at 6:00 AM. If he tried to return to work, he would be fired.

In mid November, that woman, who had been talking to that imaginary person last year, was back. She was still talking to that imaginary person. This time she was saying, "I saw you messing with my husband." She then said, "Don't lie to me, you son of a bitch." She came by the next day. She was still talking to that imaginary person. This time she said, "I saw you do that, you mother fucker." I thought, "Damn, someone needs to take her to a mental hospital. She's freaking crazy."

A few days before Thanksgiving, Sonja transfers to Long Branch. She transfers because of Marcy Joyce's big mouth. Sonja and Marcy Joyce just couldn't get along. Marcy Joyce was always mouthing at Sonja. I didn't blame Sonja one bit.

On December 1, the Burger Store hires Geoff Dybert. He turns out to be a really good worker. He also becomes a good friend of mine. A few days later, Heidi becomes store manager. Carl becomes store manager at the new Beaconville Road store.

The week before Christmas, Marcy Joyce had been pissing me off, quite a bit that day. She comes up to me, and gives me a list of things, Heidi wants me to do. Marcy Joyce hands me the list and says, "Here's the list of things Heidi wants you to do." Well, I got so mad, I ripped the list right out of her hand. Marcy Joyce was so shocked, she didn't know what to think. The one thing Heidi wanted me to do, was wash the windows. I complained right away. It was 18 degrees outside. The glass cleaner would freeze. Well, Josh Kert and I tried washing the windows. Guess what happened? The glass cleaner froze. Josh and I told Heidi, "The glass cleaner froze." Heidi gets mad and says, "I'll get Tori to do it. She could probably do it better than you." Josh and I walked away. Josh said, "We tried to tell her it would freeze." Tori tries to wash the windows. Guess what? The glass cleaner froze. Heidi was worried. There was word that Tim, might be stopping by the store. I really didn't give a shit.

The next day, Lita told me, "Whenever Heidi asks you to do something, you should do it." She then said, "Heidi has to put up with a lot of stuff, especially when Tim is at the store." When Heidi came in that morning, Lita told me, "Greg, remember what I said." I said, "Yeah." I said yeah like I didn't mean it. Lita and I always got along. However, I wasn't going to take any shit off of her.

About 2 days after Christmas, Marcy Joyce transfers to Beaconville Road. I thought, "Hot damn!" I was so glad to see her go.

Chapter 12

1997

On Saturday, January 4, someone knocked on my door at 3:30 AM. Thankfully, I was already awake. I had no idea who it could've been. I opened the door and this woman said, "Could you give me a ride home?" I (disgusted) said, "No I can't" and closed the door. I could tell that woman was stoned out of her mind. She had to have been on some kind of drug. I mean, you just don't knock on somebody's door at 3:30 AM, unless it's an emergency. Besides, I had never seen that woman before in my life. She didn't get a ride home from me. I don't have any use for people who do drugs. After I closed the door, I said to myself, "The next time someone knocks on my door at 3:30 AM, it better be Elizabeth Vargas." By the way, Elizabeth Vargas is my favorite TV news journalist. She is DEFINITELY one of the most beautiful women on TV.

As the year went on, people were started to complain about Heidi. They complained about the way she did things. A few people had quit because of her. The store immediately went downhill when Carl left.

The last Saturday in January, I had to work at Beaconville Road. They had no janitor that day. They couldn't get anyone at their store, to do janitor work. They absolutely had to have me.

A few days later, I heard Heidi talking to Doby on the phone. Doby was saying that Harriet got into it with a customer. I heard Heidi say, "Well, she's fired." Harriet did not get fired. That was just a bunch of talk.

In early February, Harriet was giving Geoff some hard times. Geoff's grandmother had been really sick at that time. Geoff's mom called and Cara Glabb, answered the phone. She told her about his grandmother.

Geoff's mom asked if he could get off early that day. Cara said he could. Geoff told Harriet that he had to leave. Harriet rolled her eyes at him. She was saying that Geoff, was trying to get out of work. Geoff did have a family emergency back in late December. He had to leave early at that time. Harriet was just mad, cause Geoff had to leave. Family was more important than the Burger Store.

Also in early February, Heidi stole money from a cash register drawer. She made it look, as if Lita stole the money. Lita noticed what Heidi did right away. Lita confronted her. Lita told her not to do that again. Heidi got the message. A week later, Heidi stole money from a cash register drawer. This time, she made it look, as if Cara stole the money. Cara would not fall for Heidi's trick. Heidi would continue to steal money from cash register drawers. She continued to make it look like, other people were stealing the money. A few people had quit because of Heidi's trickery. A few people even got fired because of it. I guess they just didn't see, what Heidi was doing.

In early March, I was putting up stock downstairs. Heidi yells downstairs at me and says, "Get up here and change the menu light." She didn't have to yell at me like that. When I got upstairs, I was so angry, I kicked an empty box. The box hit the door, that goes to the back drive-thru. Apparently, Heidi heard the box hit the door. Felicia Fentrix says, "Heidi wants to see you." I went to see what Heidi wanted. Heidi says, "If that box hits the door again, you're going home." I told her it was an accident. She said, "It didn't sound like no accident to me." Heidi then says, "I don't know what the hell is wrong with everybody here lately." I knew what was wrong. No one wanted to work for Heidi. She was not a good store manager. After she said, "You're going home," I really didn't give a damn.

In early March, the Burger Store was about to have an inspection. Doby messes up the routine, of how to serve food. Lita immediately complained to Mark. Lita was saying that Doby's way was more complicated. Mark said, "After the inspection, We'll Lita-ize it." Doby never could stick to one routine. He always had to change it. Doby's way was always complicated.

In mid March, Geoff and his fiancée were having problems. He asked Cara if he could cool off. Geoff went outside. Eva Balligan went out to talk to Geoff. Eva said, "Everything would be alright." Harriet was telling Geoff to get back to work. Geoff goes back inside. He goes downstairs to cool off more. Cara goes downstairs to see if Geoff is OK. Geoff says, "Get the fuck back." Harriet comes downstairs and yells to Geoff, "Get back to work." Geoff (angry) punches the wall. Harriet thought he hit Cara. Nonetheless, Harriet yells, "Get back to work." Geoff (angry) says, "Take Cara and your nappy ass back upstairs, and get back to work." Geoff would recover from his incident.

A few days later, the store flooded. The drains in the restrooms had backed up. Water was going into the lobby. I was taking out the trash, when the flood started. Harriet (angry) yells, "Greg, get up here." That was when I FINALLY snapped. I said to myself, "My last day is June 12, 1997."

During the third week of March, that same woman, who had been talking to that imaginary person, was back. This time she said, "You better leave me alone, or I'll knock the shit out of you." I thought, "Damn, she's crazy." During the last week of March, Heidi gets herself a brand new truck. She probably used that money she had stolen, to pay for it.

In early April, Wayne drops a gallon of mustard on the floor. It went all over Tori. I thought that was funny, because I didn't like Tori. However, Wayne did make a mess on the floor. The basement also flooded in early April. The sump pump breaks down, along with another water pipe. Surprisingly, they both get fixed that same day. There had been a lot of rain in Peddleton at that time. Several flash floods had occurred. The Weather Channel was calling for more rain. The Weather Channel was exactly right. More rain did occur. Heidi was NOT convinced that the sump pump's breaking down, caused the flood. The sump pump is what pumps the water, down the main drain. Heidi thought that all the rain, had caused the basement to flood. Heidi was afraid that the rain would cause the basement to flood again. She told me to put the pallets, on top of the soda tanks. I had to put some of the stock, on the pallets. She was afraid that some of the stock, might get damaged. She told me to leave it like that, for 3 days. Well, the basement never did flood. I did all that for nothing.

On the first Friday in April, Heidi has Wayne and me, to come in at 3:45 AM, the next day, for truck. The only thing was, truck didn't run that day. I explained to Heidi, that truck didn't run again until Monday. Heidi

1979-VARN

told me to call the Burger Store delivery warehouse, to see when the truck runs again. They said, "It runs again Monday." Heidi still has Wayne and me, to come in at 3:45 AM, the next day. Wayne and I came in early for nothing.

During the second week of April, Heidi steals money from a cash register drawer. This time, she makes it look like Sandra stole the money. Devon finds out about it, and is boiling mad. Devon was working at a local convenience store. Mark's sister, Polly, comes in the store, where Devon was working. He gives her a mouthful. Devon says, "You better do something about Heidi, or something's going to happen to her new truck." Polly said she would talk to Mark. It did no good. Heidi would continue to steal money.

In mid April, the Burger Store had been very busy at that time. The Fun Toys had arrived. The store had ordered a month's supply of Fun Toys, but they were gone in 5 days. We couldn't keep enough hamburger buns in the store. We even doubled the order of buns, but it wasn't enough. I was scheduled to be off the third Saturday in April. Heidi asked me the day before, if I wanted to work. I was going to tell her no, but before I could answer, she says, "Well, you're going to work." I went in that Saturday at 7:00 AM. Heidi had me doing all kinds of stuff. It was like I was her personal house slave. At around 9:00 AM, she got some money from the store safe. This time she wasn't stealing. She gave me that money to go to a local bakery store, and buy every package of hamburger buns that they had. The bread truck didn't run that day. The store was out of buns. Later that day, the store was out of Large Burger containers. Heidi called the Peddleton Mall to see if they had any they could loan us. Irby Baneer, the swing manager said they had plenty. When I got there, Irby said, "They can't keep janitors around here." I told him, "They're going to be looking for one when June 12 gets here." Irby (surprised) said, "You're quitting?" I said, "Yes I am." Irby says, "I thought you were one of their permanent fixtures." I (angry) said, "Well, you thought wrong." Irby was shocked. I grabbed the Large Burger containers and left. That day, I was in no mood for anybody's shit.

During the third week of April, LeRon was accused of stealing a car and possession of marijuana. However, it was not LeRon. It was his twin brother, DeRon. Doby finds out about it and takes LeRon off the schedule. LeRon was cleared of all charges. DeRon was captured. LeRon explained to Doby about what happened. Doby would not let LeRon return to work. In other words, he was fired. LeRon was a good worker.

During the last day of April, Lita said something about Tim, coming by the store. I said, "Well, tell him to get his ass on in here." I said, "June 12 is my last day anyway." I said, "He's just a person." Wayne had also said something about Tim, coming by the store. I just said, "Tell him to get his ass on in here." I was taking the Stone Cold Steve Austin approach to that situation. He would have probably said the same thing.

During the first week of May, Harlan Caffren had gotten a hold of some Fun Toys. There are many different stories to this episode. I'm not really sure which one is true. Harlan says that he bought a couple of cases of Fun Toys. He said that a local business was wanting to buy a couple of cases. I heard somebody say that Harlan had hi-jacked a truck, that was carrying Fun Toys. Ward got word that Harlan had something to do with Fun Toys. Ward suspected that Harlan stole the Fun Toys from the store. Harlan denied it. Janece Broxson says she saw Harlan selling Fun Toys at a local shopping center. Janece said that Harlan had his own little stand, where he was selling them. Lita told me that Harlan finally admitted, that he stole the Fun Toys. He was fired a few days later. I never found out what really happened though.

On Mother's Day, the first thing I did was, put in my 2 weeks notice. The note said, "Heidi, my last day is June 12. I have found another job." I really didn't have another job. However, I did have a lead on one job. That day, I started counting down to my last day. At around 9:30 AM, Sean Balligan went into a violent rage. I was washing dishes. All of a sudden, Sean starts cussing and throwing down utensils. He was threatening to beat up a customer. Sean had gotten mad because that customer had asked for fresh pancakes. Sean said, "Beggars can't be choosers." Apparently, that customer said something to Sean. Both Sean and the customer act like they were going to fight each other. Sean throws a box at the customer, but misses. Heidi tells Melinda Kurden to call the police. The police arrive in a few minutes. They immediately calm down Sean and the customer. The police asked Sean and the customer a few questions, and then left. I said to myself, "Well, Sean just lost his job." Harriet (angry) says, "Sean, go home." Sean knew he was going to get sent home anyway. Harriet just had to open her big mouth. Sean did go home. However, he returned an hour and a half later. In other words, Sean did not get fired. I thought, "Damn!" Most places would have fired someone for doing what Sean did. Like I've said many times before, the Burger Store was very desperate for workers. Lita told me that customer had always asked for fresh pancakes. It didn't matter if he had to wait 10 or 15 minutes.

A week later, Heidi finds out that I'm quitting. She immediately starts asking me why I'm quitting. She asked me where I found another job. I told her, "At a construction company." She asked, "Which one?" I said, "Skip Wullard." Skip had his own brick laying business. I told her that to get her off my back.

The day after Memorial Day, Lita told me that Heidi wanted me to go outside, and pull weeds. I said, "But it's raining." Lita said, "I know." Heidi said that Mark stopped by yesterday and complained about weeds. Lita said, "The reason why Heidi is making you pull weeds in the rain is, because you're quitting." I went out to pull weeds. The only thing was, I pulled them where it was roofed over. That way I wouldn't get wet. I was very close to walking out that day. I thought, "June 12 is not far away. Heidi is going on vacation for 2 weeks, starting June 2." Although, I still had a lead on that one job, there was no guarantee I was going to get it. I wanted to make sure I had a good check when I left.

The next morning, Lita told me that Janece had been telling Heidi a few things about me. Janece told Heidi that I was counting down until my last day. Lita tells me that Heidi made a comment concerning me. Heidi said, "Well, Greg may be leaving sooner than he thinks." I told Lita, "If Heidi fires me, I'll just go on unemployment for a while." Lita told me to watch what I say to people. I simply didn't care. I was getting ready to quit anyway. What difference did it make? I think Lita was trying to talk me out of quitting. It wasn't going to work.

During the first week of June, Mark and Doby had FINALLY gotten word that Heidi, had been stealing money from the store. They had stopped by those first 3 days that week. Mark and Doby were doing a big time investigation. They found that Heidi had been stealing money left and right. It came up on the shift reports and paperwork. She even stole a check from a church group. The check was worth about $125. The church had paid for some food a week earlier. Heidi pocketed the check herself. When I think back to all those money shortages back in 1995, now I know who was taking that money. It was Heidi.

On June 3, Geoff had a virus that day. He wasn't able to work. It was also payday. Geoff calls the store and talks to Cara. He told her that his mom, Sharon, would pick up his paycheck. Cara said that would be OK. Cara told Harriet that Geoff's mom, Sharon, would be by to get Geoff's check. When Sharon stopped by to get his check, Harriet said that she couldn't give her his check. Sharon even showed identification. Harriet still would not give her Geoff's check. Sharon called Geoff and explained the situation. Geoff, not feeling good, shows up to get his check. Geoff says to Harriet, "Cara told you that my mom would pick up my check." Harriet said, "Oh! I forgot." Harriet gives Geoff his check. Harriet then says, "Get the fuck out of my store." About a second later, a customer walks to the counter. Harriet says, "Get the fuck out of my store." Well, that did it for Geoff. The next day, Geoff went by the store, and got Doby's phone number. He called Doby that same day. Doby showed up, and Geoff explained what had happened. Doby said he would talk to Harriet. After Geoff was finished talking to Doby, Geoff had to wait for his ride. The funny thing was, he was waiting by Harriet's car. Harriet said that Geoff needed to calm down, and get a grip on his attitude. Geoff said to Harriet, "You need to get a grip before I do. Your attitude is worse than mine." Harriet would not go up to Geoff, and say what she said. She was probably afraid Geoff might attack her.

One week before my last day, Lita tries to talk me into staying. She said, "Why don't you go ahead and stay?" I said, "No thanks." Lita said that Heidi will be fired, when she gets back from vacation. I said, "No thanks, I've made my decision." The next day, Sandra tries to talk me into staying. She asked me if I was sure I was quitting. I told her, "Yes I am." Sandra says, "What if Mark was to give you a raise?" I said, "Mark's not going to give me a raise." Sandra says, "I wouldn't be so sure." Sandra said, "You're quitting because of Heidi, right?" I said, "Well, yeah." I then told Sandra, "There are a lot more reasons why I am quitting, not just because of Heidi." Sandra told Mark that I was quitting. Mark was not happy. Sandra asked Mark about the time Heidi, wanted me to pull weeds in the rain. Mark said that he had not complained about weeds. Heidi made the whole thing up. Sandra felt that Heidi would be fired as well. I told Sandra, "I don't think Heidi will be fired." Sandra's plan didn't work.

The Monday before my last day, Judd stopped by the store. I told him, "This Thursday is my last day." He asked me if I had another job. I said, "No, but I had a good lead on one." He said, "You might be making a mistake." I told Judd, "Don't worry, I'll be fine." The next day, rumors were going around the store. Those rumors were about me. People were saying that I was going to get that job, I had a lead on. They said that I would not like it, and would return to the Burger Store. I ignored those rumors. I was sticking to my word.

Before I get to my last day, I would like to tell you, all the things that happened over the years. Those are the things that just kept happening, over and over again. Some of them until my last day. Night shift would always wash the grill towels and regular towels together. That was a no-no. The sump pump would get stopped up, and the basement would flood. That happened at least 4 or 5 times a year. Wayne continued to have a habit of not having food in the bin by 6:00 AM (opening time). Wayne would continue to drop things. He would make mess after mess. Sometimes he was called, "butterfingers." Wayne would continue to eat hot dogs almost everyday. The one thing that Wayne would always do, was copy the things I liked. He didn't like the Oakland Raiders, until he found out I liked them. He didn't like LeAnn Rimes, until he found out I liked her. Doby continued to change the routine of how food was served. He never could stick to one routine. He would always change the routine every week or two. Doby was always trying to tell me, and everyone else, how to do their jobs. I said to myself during my last week, "If he tells me how to do my job, he's going to get told off." Fortunately, Doby didn't try. I was almost always, having to get ice, for the front counter. Even though there were several people working front counter, I still had to get ice. I hardly ever got raises when it was time for one. One time, I didn't get a raise for nearly 2 years. Certain people got away with certain things. If I would have done what those certain people did, I would have probably gotten fired. A lot of times, Judd would stand out on the back sidewalk. He would drink coffee and smoke a cigarette. I know he made 9 or 10 dollars an hour. One time I said to myself, "I wish I had a job like that." I'm sure there was work Judd had to do. Then again, he was lazy. Judd told me one time that Lyle, would give him a job to do. He would give the other store office guys jobs also. Lyle would always explain how long those jobs would take. Lyle would say for example, "This job will take half a day. This job will take a day. This job will take a day and a half. This job will take 2 days." Mark wanted all those jobs done in a day. However, when Lyle would stop by the store, he would always gripe about something. Although, I didn't like Lyle, I did have respect for him. He was born poor. He worked very hard to have 5 Burger Stores. There were other Burger Stores, but they were Mark's stores. All Mark did, was inherit the other Burger Stores. A lot of times over the years, things would make me really angry. There were times when I lost my temper really bad. There were times when I went into purple face frenzies. A few people were surprised that I didn't get fired, for losing my temper like I did. I told them, "The Burger Store didn't have the guts to fire me." I was one of their best workers ever. Well, my last day, June 12, was finally here. Everything went really well that day. Although, Eva said something to me, that I didn't like. She said, "Greg, I think you're making a mistake by quitting." I told her, "The mistake would be for me to stay here." I was getting no where working at the Burger Store. They had no retirement plans or pensions. At 12 noon, Doby told me, "Come back and work for the Burger Store anytime." I told him, "No thanks." Well, 1:00 PM had arrived. It was the end of an era. The sad thing was, when I left, I was only making $5.85 an hour. I guess Millionaire Mark was too cheap, to pay me more money.

Even though I didn't work at the Burger Store anymore, my name was still turning up in conversations. There were rumors circulating, that I was coming back. I stuck to my word. I did NOT return. Harriet FINALLY got demoted. It happened a week after I quit. Doby FINALLY had enough complaints about her. I thought, "What the hell took you so long?" She was also transferred to Beaconville Road. Although, Harriet still wore manager clothes, they probably couldn't find any regular employee clothes that would fit her. Heidi did NOT get fired. I repeat, Heidi did

NOT get fired. She got demoted to assistant manager at Beaconville Road. That happened 2 and a half weeks after I quit. The word fired, according to the dictionary means, "To be dismissed from employment." The word fired, according to the Burger Store means, "To be transferred or demoted, or both." I tried to tell everybody that Heidi wouldn't get fired, but they wouldn't listen. Everybody was fooled except me. Well, about 2 weeks after I quit, the Burger Store started hiring people in at $6 an hour. Well, that made me absolutely sick. It took my quitting for Millionaire Mark, to start people at $6 an hour. A few people said that my quitting, had nothing to do with Mark, starting people at $6 an hour. My quitting had everything to do with it. Millionaire Mark never would pay me $6 an hour, even after I had been there 11 years, 9 months, and 5 days.

Author Bio This is my first book I hope to write more books in the near future. My next book will be a fictional drama. I was born in Illinois but I have lived most of my life in Western Kentucky, where I still live today. Address

Greg Tate P.O. Box 161 Melber, Ky 42069-0161

1979-VARN

Printed in the United States
26167LVS00001B/53

9 780738 829845